The Life of Muhammad

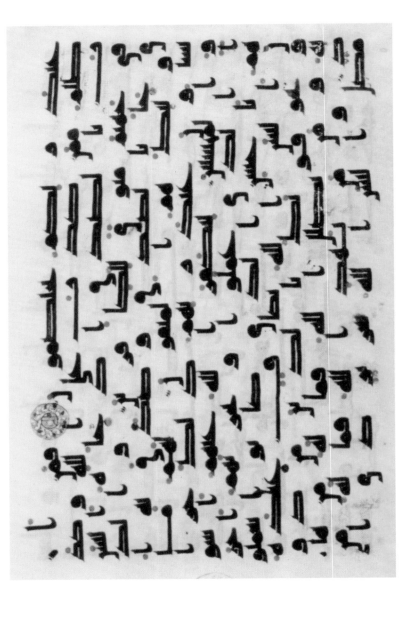

IBN ISHAQ

THE LIFE OF
MUHAMMAD
Apostle of Allah

—

EDITED BY
Michael Edwardes

London
THE FOLIO SOCIETY
2003

© Copyright The Folio Society Limited 1964

This edited edition of Edward Rehatsek's translation
of *The Life of Muhammad* is published by courtesy
of the Royal Asiatic Society, London

First published by The Folio Society in 1964
Reprinted (with a new binding and frontispiece) 2003

Eighth printing 2006

Map redrawn by Reginald Piggott

The frontispiece shows a detail from
a page of a ninth-century Kufic Koran
from the Near East, Iraq or Persia.
(The British Library / Or 1399, fo. 1r)

Set in 'Monotype' Imprint
Printed in Great Britain at the Bath Press
on Abbey Wove paper and bound
by them in full buckram

CONTENTS

INTRODUCTION

IT is always extremely difficult to be objective about the life of the founder of a great religion – his personality is inevitably blurred by an aura of the miraculous. Early biographers are preoccupied, not with historical fact, but with glorifying in every way the memory of one they believe to have been a Messenger of God or even God Himself. Consequently, there is a rich accretion of myth and miracle, mysterious portents and heavenly signs, of residues from other religious beliefs and traditions, the propaganda, in fact, of an expanding faith. All these will be found in the biography of Muhammad which follows. But behind the legendary Muhammad there lies one of the great figures of history, and, although very little is known about his early years – the first certain date being that of the migration from Mecca to Medina, which took place in AD 622 – it is possible to build up the events of his real, as distinct from his symbolic, life.

Muhammad was born at Mecca about AD 570 into a poor family of the Quraysh tribe. When he was twenty-five years of age he was employed by Khadija, a wealthy widow, to go with one of her trading caravans to Syria. On the successful completion of the journey, Muhammad married Khadija, who was some fifteen years older than he. Two sons and four daughters were born of this marriage. The two boys died in infancy, but one of the daughters, Fatima, married Muhammad's cousin Ali, and it is the descendants of Fatima and Ali who are said to be the true heirs of the Prophet.

The community Muhammad was born into was pagan, the gods often being represented by stones. One of the most important places of pilgrimage was the sanctuary of the Kaba, in which was a black stone, at Mecca. Scattered about Arabia at this time were communities of Jews and Christians, whose belief in only one god was to influence Muhammad when he came to state his own religious ideas. How he learned of these beliefs during the fifteen years between the date of his marriage to Khadija and the revelation of the first divine communication is not known, but there were many Arab converts to Judaism and Christianity and, as Muhammad grew more and more dissatisfied with the pagan gods, it is obvious that he must have investigated the religions of those who claimed to worship the one true god.

Muhammad was in the habit of spending periods in meditation on Mount Hira, near Mecca, and there in his fortieth year he is supposed to have received his first revelation from God. The communication terrified him and he spoke of it and of a number of others which followed only to Khadija and a few close friends. But finally he received a command to proclaim publicly what had been revealed to him. Most of his family had scornfully rejected his teaching and his early converts were slaves and people of the lower classes. His preaching soon drew not only mockery but active opposition from the people of Mecca, who believed that his mission threatened their position as guardians of the Kaba, a position which brought them great wealth from the pilgrim traffic. The Meccans tried to discredit him, charging him with sorcery and with stealing his ideas from Jews and Christians. From opposition to persecution was but a step. A hundred of his followers emigrated to Abyssinia, and finally Muhammad himself decided to leave Mecca and went to Medina in AD 622. From this year the Muslim Era is dated.

INTRODUCTION

From a persecuted religious teacher in Mecca, Muhammad in Medina became the leader of a religious community and was acknowledged to be the messenger of God. He still, however, had doubters and enemies. The Jews, whom he had hoped would welcome him, were among his bitterest opponents. His assumption of authority at Medina was also resented by some of that city's leading men. Nevertheless, by careful diplomacy and firmness of purpose, he began to create a brotherhood of the faith, transcending all other ties and relationships, even those of father and son. This brotherhood united all Muslims by giving them a common purpose – the defence of the faith – and made God, and His prophet, the final source of law.

This achieved, Muhammad began to look outward, not only because he wished to convert all Arabs to his teaching, but also in an attempt to alleviate growing economic distress in Medina. Muhammad's first step was to persuade the Medinans that they must attack Mecca. This was, in fact, the first test of the new brotherhood, for many of those in Medina had relatives in Mecca and to the Arabs the ties of blood were sacred. Muhammad, however, insisted that war was a sacred duty, demanded by Allah, and he was finally able to persuade his followers that this was so. Muhammad first sent parties to attack the caravans of Mecca on their journeys to or from Syria. One attack was carried out during the sacred month of Rajab (January 624), when war was banned throughout Arabia. In the Koran, Muhammad justified this break with tradition by claiming that there could be no scruples in the fight to overcome idolatry.

From this time onwards events moved rapidly. Two months later a battle took place at Badr between three hundred Muslims and nearly a thousand Meccans. The former were triumphant, taking many prisoners. Soon after, Muhammad began a series of campaigns to expel the Jews from around Medina. These campaigns were interrupted firstly by an attack by the Meccans, in which the Muslims were defeated at Uhud, and then by an unsuccessful Meccan attempt to besiege Medina. After the Meccans had retired, Muhammad dealt with the last Jewish tribe near Medina which had supported the Meccans. The men were killed and the women and children enslaved.

Muhammad now began to subdue the tribes surrounding Mecca, and the result was a ten-year truce permitting the Muslims to return to Mecca for the yearly pilgrimage to the Kaba. After this, adherents flowed in and, though the prophet only lived four more years, in that time the future of the countries of the Near East was to be determined for hundreds of years to come. The attacks on Jewish tribes continued and much of the wealth of the country, which had previously been monopolized by Jewish traders and landowners, was seized by the Muslims. From a despised minority the followers of Muhammad were now becoming the most powerful single force in Arabia.

The truce was broken by the Meccans in AD 630, when the Quraysh attacked a tribe under Muslim protection. Muhammad marched on Mecca and occupied the city with very little opposition. The prophet showed great magnanimity in dealing with his opponents and only four people were put to death after the capture of the city, though one was a singing-girl who had composed satirical verses about Muhammad. He was now accepted as the apostle of God. Soon his armies were moving out to areas occupied by Christians, but an expedition against the Byzantines was soundly defeated. Deputations, however, came to pay him homage and there were so many that the year 9 of the *hijra* (AD 631) is known as the Year of Deputations. But the prophet had not much longer to live. He died at Medina on 8 June 632.

There is no doubt that Muslims are right when they date the beginning of an era from the prophet's migration to Medina in 622. In Mecca, Muhammad had been merely a preacher of unpopular doctrine. In Medina, however, he found a centre from which to propagate a new religion. In organizing a community of believers, Muhammad gradually established religious, social and political laws, and from them produced a distinct religious system. The system was all-embracing, and from it emerged something like a totalitarian state, with Allah as the universal king and His prophet ruling in His name. Muhammad, though preaching compassion and mercy, sometimes acted cruelly, but he must be judged within the context of his times and none of his contemporaries criticized his actions on moral grounds. He was a man of extraordinary powers and he must have had great personal charm, for he was able to attract and keep the devotion of men of widely differing types. Within a century of his death the cry 'Allah is most great!' was to be heard from Spain to China. Today, over two hundred million people in the Near East and Africa, in South and South-east Asia, still listen to the same call to prayer that was first heard in the remote Arabian desert thirteen centuries ago.

The followers of Muhammad, like the followers of Christ, are 'People of the Book'. The Bible of the Christians was once believed to be the literal word of God. Today, modern research has made this difficult to accept. To the Muslims, however, the doctrine of God's infallible word is a fundamental article of faith and very few have ever questioned it. The sacred book which contains the word of God is called the Koran. The actual words were given to Muhammad by an angel, Gabriel, over a period of some twenty years, firstly in Mecca and then in Medina. Muhammad, who is said to have been unable to read and write, repeated the angel's words from memory and they were either written down or memorized by his followers. After the death of the prophet, Abu Bakr, his successor as Caliph of Islam, commissioned the prophet's secretary Zayd to make the first collection of the Koran. The final form was reached under the third Caliph, Uthman.

The Koran is divided into 114 chapters, called *suras*. They are not chronologically arranged, and only occasionally is there a clue as to when the words were spoken or upon what occasion. The arrangement is based upon length, the longest *suras* first and the shortest, last. For many hundreds of years scholars have been trying to relate individual *suras* to particular periods of Muhammad's life, but until the same scientific treatment that has been given to the Christian Bible is given to the Koran no great progress can be expected.

The contents of the Koran can be divided under four main heads: (1) Those passages concerning the worship of the one god, Allah, the creator of all things, and from whom all that is good flows. (2) Passages concerned with the doctrine of death, resurrection, judgement, and the rewards of heaven and hell. The delights of paradise are very considerable. There, beautiful girls and youths minister to the pleasures of believers; but hell is black smoke and terrible heat. (3) Stories of earlier messengers of God, most of them Jewish and derived from the Old Testament. (4) Proclamations and regulations, mainly from the Medina period. The laws expounded show the influence of Judaism and Christianity, but are in many cases adaptations of old Arab customs.

The chief religious duties laid down by the Koran are prayer, alms-giving, fasting and pilgrimage. Prayer is the 'key to paradise' and requires religious purifications, bathing before prayer, and so on. 'The practice of religion being founded on cleanliness', the ground upon which the believer prays must also be clean and a special prayer-carpet is suggested. There are five prayers every twenty-four hours, and the face of the worshipper must be turned towards Mecca.

Alms were originally collected by the ruler and were supposed to represent one-fortieth of a man's income in money or kind. Today, however, it is left to the conscience of the individual.

The third duty is fasting. This is based upon Christian and Jewish practices and is specifically stated to be so in the Koran. The month of Ramadan, which does not fall at the same season every year – since the Muslim calendar is a lunar one – often occurs in the hottest time of the year and, in consequence, imposes very considerable strains on Muslims. During the fast, eating, drinking, smoking, smelling perfumes, bathing, and all other worldly pleasures are forbidden between sunrise and sunset. None except the sick, travellers, and soldiers in time of war, are exempt, and they must fast an equal number of days at some other time in recompense. Nurses and pregnant women need not fast at all.

The last of the principal – and binding – duties is that of

pilgrimage. Every Muslim, unless prevented by sickness or
poverty, is expected to make the pilgrimage to Mecca once in his
life. There he must walk around the Kaba seven times, kiss the
black stone set in one of its walls, run between the two hills of
Safa and Marwa near by, travel to Arafat, a hill some twelve
miles from Mecca, and on the way back sacrifice sheep and
camels at Mina, where a ceremonial stoning of devils takes place.

These four duties plus the profession of faith in Allah and
Muhammad, His prophet, are known as the five 'Pillars of the
Faith'.

Among the many other ordinances contained in the Koran
is a prohibition against alcohol, as giving rise to 'more evil than
good'. Pork is also forbidden, and animals must be slaughtered
according to fixed rules. Idolatry is an unforgivable sin and the
laws against the making of images and pictures are particularly
stringent. Anyone who makes an imitation of any living thing
will, on the day of judgement, undergo punishment in hell for
a certain period of time. Usury is prohibited and all forms of
gambling are condemned. Slavery is recognized, but slaves
must be kindly treated and even encouraged to purchase their
liberty. Women slaves may be taken as concubines.

The Koran has much to say about the position of women.
That position is implicitly defined by the word for marriage,
which is the same as that used for the sexual act. A man may
have four wives and any number of concubines, but all his wives
must be treated equally. A man may divorce his wife, but a
woman cannot divorce her husband. The Koran specifically
states that women are inferior to men.

An injunction to fight the infidel guarantees to those who die
in defence of Islam the reward of martyrdom and entry into
paradise. People of different faiths on whom war is declared are
first to be offered the choice: to embrace Islam; to pay tribute,
in which case they may continue to practise their faith; or to
settle the affair by the fortunes of war, in which case captives
are made slaves, the men usually being slain unless they embrace
Islam. One-fifth part of any spoil belongs to the ruler.

The ethical teaching of the Koran is high and it may be said to represent a sort of mercantile theology, emerging as it does from the commercial background of Muhammad and the Arabs. It was the duty of an Arab in Muhammad's time to support his tribe, to give food and shelter to the traveller, and to protect those who claimed his protection. Commerce was impossible without good faith and honest dealing. To these precepts Muhammad gave a religious sanction and offered in return rewards according to each man's deeds. But the appeal is not only to self-interest. It is God who hates injustice and oppression, and who is above all compassionate and merciful; man has the responsibility and the power to be the same.

The present life of Muhammad is by the earliest biographer whose work has survived. Ibn Ishaq was born in Medina about eighty-five years after the *hijra* (AH 85) and died in Baghdad in AH 151. No copy of Ibn Ishaq's biography in its original form is now in existence, but it was extensively quarried by Ibn Hisham (died AH 213 or 218). Much of the material used was left in the original words and in whole sections, so that Ibn Hisham's work can best be described as an edited version of the original biography, with interpolations by the editor.

Ishaq's work is not a biography in the modern sense, but more a compilation of anecdotes and traditions collected by him and arranged in chronological periods. Collected within a century of the prophet's death, it bears the stamp of authenticity, though again not in a modern sense. The miraculous is always present and is given the same weight as mundane descriptions of the prophet's actions. Because tales of miracles may be unacceptable today, this does not mean that other parts of the biography are untrustworthy. The facts are there, and the miraculous is that essential embroidery of faith which the life of no religious leader – from Christ to the Buddha – is without.

The translation which follows is the first known English version of Ibn Ishaq's biography, and is here published for the first time. The translator, Edward Rehatsek, was born in Hungary in 1819 and died in Bombay in 1891. He arrived in India in 1847 and spent a number of years in research upon oriental

INTRODUCTION

subjects. He later became professor of mathematics and Latin at Wilson College, Bombay, from which position he retired in 1871. Rehatsek lived the life of a recluse, working upon his translations from Arabic and many other languages. After his death, his body was burned in the Hindu manner, the first European, it is said, to be cremated in India. The manuscript of the translation was completed just before his death and was presented to the Royal Asiatic Society, London, by F. F. Arbuthnot, the Islamic scholar, in 1898. This edition is published by courtesy of the Society.

The original work is extremely long, over a thousand pages of the translator's small yet clear handwriting. Rehatsek produced an almost literal translation and it suffers somewhat from scholarly pedanticism. In preparing this edition for publication, I have kept one main aim in view – to present the earliest extant life of Muhammad in a form, and at a length, acceptable to the general reader. To do this it has been necessary to cut the text as well as to make some rearrangement in the interests of orderly chronology. I have inserted linking passages, printed in italic, where the text seems to require it. Generally speaking, those parts which have been excised have been repetitions of events, long lists of names, confusing accounts of minor battles, and a large quantity of verse. Some errors have been corrected and verbal infelicities removed. The transliteration of Arabic names is always something of a problem in books intended for the reader who has no knowledge of Eastern languages. In this instance I have omitted all diacritical marks, believing it preferable for the reader to mispronounce the words rather than be prevented from pronouncing them at all by the intrusion of apostrophes and other symbols.

MICHAEL EDWARDES

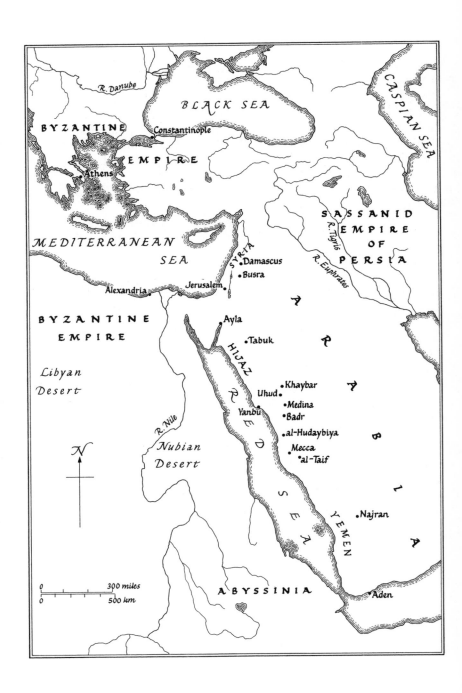

THE LIFE OF
MUHAMMAD

THE EARLY LIFE OF THE APOSTLE OF ALLAH

IT is recorded that when the mother of the apostle of Allah became pregnant with him she had a vision, and a voice spoke to her, saying, 'Thou art pregnant with the prince of this nation. When he is born on this earth, thou must say, "I place him under the protection of the only One, from the wickedness of every envious person." And thou must name him Muhammad.'

While she was carrying the child in her womb she saw a light issue from her which illuminated even the castles of Busra in Syria. And Abdullah b. Abdul-Muttalib, the father of the apostle, died while the child was yet unborn.

The apostle of Allah was born on a Monday, on the thirteenth day of the month of Rabi in the year of the Elephant [c. 570].*
At the time of the apostle's birth a Jew standing on the flat roof of a house in Medina called forth the Jewish people and when they assembled around him, saying, 'Woe to you. What is the

*The year of an invasion by the Abyssinians, whose army was made memorable in Arabia by having an elephant in its train.

matter?' he told them 'This night the star has risen, under which the apostle is born.'

When his mother was delivered of the apostle of Allah she sent the following message to his grandfather: 'An infant is born to you; come and see him.' He came and she informed him of what she had seen and heard during her pregnancy and the name she had been ordered to give the child. It is said that his grandfather took the boy into the Kaba [place of worship] and prayed to Allah and thanked Him for His gift; then he brought him again to his mother. Soon he hired for the boy a nurse, whose name was Halima.

Halima was the daughter of Abu Dhuayb of the Banu Sad tribe. The tradition concerning her is that she went forth with her husband and a little son whom she was suckling, with others of the women of the Banu Sad who were in search of children to nurse. She relates: 'In a year of dearth, when nothing was left us, I went forth on a piebald she-ass and we had with us a she-camel which gave us not one drop of milk. We could not sleep the whole night, because the infant we had with us cried for hunger, there being nothing in my breasts to satisfy him nor anything in our camel to nourish him. We were, however, hoping for aid and deliverance; accordingly I continued the journey, riding on my she-ass which was so weak that it lagged behind and the people complained.

'At last, we arrived in Mecca to look for sucklings, and there was not a woman among us to whom the apostle of Allah was not offered. They all refused to take charge of him as soon as they were told that he was an orphan, because we expected benefits from the father of an infant but did not like orphans, thinking that a mother or a grandfather would do us but little good. Not a woman, however, remained who had not obtained a suckling except myself. When we assembled to depart, I said to my husband, "I am unwilling to return with my companions and not take a suckling. I shall go to that orphan and take it." He replied, "Do so! Perhaps Allah will make it a blessing to us." Then I went and took him just because I could find no other child.

'After that, I took him to my arms and offered him my breast and he drank as much as he liked till he was satisfied, and his milk-brother did the same till he had enough. After that both of them slept, whereas before we could not sleep for our child wailing. Then my husband approached our she-camel, and lo! it was full. Accordingly I milked it, and we both drank until we were satisfied and filled, so that we had a good night. In the morning, my husband said, "By Allah, Halima, you have brought a blessed soul." I replied "This is just what I hope for." After that we departed. I mounted my she-ass with the infant, but the animal ran so fast that the other donkeys were not able to keep up with it, and my companions asked, "O daughter of Abu Dhuayb, is not this the same donkey on which you came?" I replied, "Yes. It is the very same", and they exclaimed, "There is something the matter with it!" When we arrived at our habitation in the country of the Banu Sad – a more sterile land than which I do not know on the earth of Allah – our sheep met me in the evening, filled with milk so that we had only to milk and drink, whereas others could not milk a single drop. And those of our people who were present said to their shepherds, "Woe to you! Pasture where the shepherd of the daughter of Abu Dhuayb is pasturing." Nevertheless their sheep returned in the evening hungry, without a drop of milk, and my sheep were filled with milk.

'In this manner we continued to receive from Allah increase and benefits for two years; then I weaned the boy and he had become strong as no other boys had. We returned him to his mother, although we were anxious that he should remain with us since we had seen the blessing he brought. I asked his mother to leave him with us to grow fat, and told her that I feared the climate and disease in Mecca might harm him. We did not cease to importune her until she allowed us to take him back.

'It was not longer than a month after our return that his milk-brother came running to me and his father, saying, "Two men dressed in white garments have taken hold of my brother, and have thrown him on the ground. They ripped open his belly, and are squeezing him." I and his foster-father hastened out and found him standing apparently unharmed but with his countenance quite altered. We questioned him, and he said, "Two men dressed in white garments came to me, who threw me down, opened my abdomen and searched in it for I know not what." We returned with him to our tent, and his foster-father said to me, "O Halima! I fear something *has* happened to the boy. Carry him to his family ere the injury becomes apparent!"

'Accordingly, we took him back to his mother, who asked, "What has brought you here, when you were so anxious that he should remain with you?" I replied, "Allah has caused my son to grow and I have done my duty, but I feared that something might befall him and therefore I have brought him back to you as you desired." She said, "Such is not the case! Tell me the truth about it." And she would not let me alone until I had told her everything. Then she asked, "Are you afraid that he is possessed by Satan?" and I replied, "Yes." She said, "No, by Allah! Satan has no access to him, because something great is the matter with my son. Shall I tell you about it? While I was pregnant with him, I saw a light issuing from me and, by Allah, I could not have had a pregnancy which was easier or lighter than this. When he was born, he placed his hands on the ground and raised his head to heaven. Do not trouble yourself about him, and return home." '

Later, the apostle of Allah himself described what had happened. 'Whilst I and my milk-brother were pasturing some animals in the rear of our house, two men came to us dressed in white garments and bearing a golden platter full of snow. They took hold of me, opened my belly, extracted my heart, split it open and took out of it a black lump of blood which they threw away. Then they washed my heart and belly with snow, until they had purified them. Then one of them said to his companion, "Weigh him against one hundred of his people." And he weighed me with them, but I proved heavier than they. Then he said, "Weigh him with one thousand of his people." This he also did, and I was again found more heavy. After that he said, "Leave him; for if you were to weigh him against his whole nation, he would outweigh it." ' Later, the apostle of Allah was in the habit of saying that there was not a prophet who had not pastured sheep.

According to their traditions, the people believe – but Allah knows best – that when his nurse brought him back to Mecca, she lost him amongst the crowd while she was taking him to his family. She searched, but could not find him again, and she went to his grandfather, Abdul-Muttalib, and said, 'I have arrived this night with Muhammad, but while I was in the upper part of the city he strayed from me, and I know not where he is.' The grandfather of Muhammad stood up near the Kaba and prayed to Allah to restore the boy, and it is believed that he was found by two men of his own tribe who brought him to Abdul-Muttalib with the words, 'Here is your son. We found him in the upper part of Mecca.' Then his grandfather took him and, making him ride on his back, walked round the Kaba, recommending him to Allah and praying for him. After that he sent him to his mother, Amina.

The apostle of Allah and his mother and his grandfather were under the protection and keeping of Allah, and the boy grew like a prosperous plant on account of the grace for which He had predestined him. When the apostle had attained his sixth year his mother Amina died in the place called Abwa, between Mecca and Medina, when she was returning to Mecca with him from a visit to his uncles. The apostle of Allah remained with his grandfather, Abdul-Muttalib.

It was usual to place a bed for Abdul-Muttalib in the shade of the Kaba, around which his sons sat until he arrived; none of his sons ventured to sit on the bed, from respect towards him. Once the apostle of Allah, who was a plump boy, came and sat down on it, and they pushed him away. When Abdul-Muttalib saw this, he said, 'Let my son alone! By Allah, he will become something great.' Then he made the boy sit down by his side on the bed, and allowed him to stroke his back with his hands, and whatever he did pleased Abdul-Muttalib. But when the apostle of Allah had attained his eighth year his grandfather died.

Abdul-Muttalib had been the acknowledged leader of the Quraysh tribe, guardians of the holy city of Mecca. When he died none of his many sons was influential enough to succeed him and leadership and influence began to pass to the descendants of his cousin, Umayya, who had long been envious of the power wielded by Abdul-Muttalib.

After the death of his grandfather, the apostle of Allah lived with his uncle Abu Talib, to whose care Abdul-Muttalib is believed to have entrusted him because Abu Talib and the father of the apostle were brothers by the same father and mother.

A soothsayer came once to Mecca to prophesy to the Quraysh and they brought their sons to him to hear his prophecies. Abu Talib visited this man, who looked at the apostle of Allah, but was then diverted from him. When the soothsayer was again at leisure, he asked for the boy and wanted to see him; but when Abu Talib perceived the man's anxiety he took his nephew away. The soothsayer exclaimed, 'Woe to you! Bring back the boy whom I have just seen; for, by Allah, he will have high dignity.' But Abu Talib would not return.

On another occasion Abu Talib went with a caravan on a trading journey to Syria. When he was about to depart the apostle of Allah clung to him, and it is believed that Abu Talib was so touched by this that he exclaimed, 'By Allah! I shall take him with me, and we shall never be separated from each other.' Accordingly he took the boy with him.

Now, at Busra, in Syria, there was a monk named Bahira who was of the Christian faith. He had always lived in the same hermitage, which possessed a book – for the instruction of the monks – which was passed down and was always kept by the oldest among them. When the caravan encamped in the vicinity of Bahira's hermitage – and they had previously often passed by without his speaking or presenting himself to them – he prepared a great deal of food for them, reputedly because of something he had seen whilst in his cell. It was said that, from his hermitage, he had seen the apostle of Allah in the caravan, and that as the caravan approached a cloud hung over the apostle of Allah. When the caravan arrived the people halted under a tree near the cell of the hermit, and he saw the cloud overshadow the tree, and the branches bent themselves over the apostle of Allah so as to protect him.

When Bahira saw this he came down from his cell and ordered food to be prepared. When it was ready he sent the following message to the people of the caravan, 'I have made a dinner for you, o ye Quraysh people. I should like you all to come, the small and the big, the bondmen and the free!' One man among them replied, 'By Allah, Bahira! There is something the matter with you today, because you have not acted thus with us before, although we passed often near you! What is the matter with you now?' Bahira replied, 'You have spoken the truth. But you are guests and I should like to honour you, and give a dinner to all of you.' Accordingly they all assembled, but the apostle of Allah remained under the tree, because of his extreme youth, with the baggage of the people. When Bahira looked around and missed him, he said, 'O, ye Quraysh people! Leave no one of you behind, deprived of my food.' They replied, 'No one who ought to come has remained behind, except a boy, and he is the youngest of the people and therefore has been left with our baggage.' Bahira said, 'Do not treat him in this way, but call him to dine with you,' and one of the Quraysh exclaimed, 'I swear by al-Lat and by al-Uzza that we are at fault for excluding the son of Abdullah from partaking with us of this dinner!' Then he went to him, brought him in his arms, and seated him among the people. When Bahira saw him he scrutinized him closely and examined him to find the signs he sought.

When the people had finished eating and dispersed Bahira addressed the apostle of Allah as follows, 'I adjure you by al-Lat and by al-Uzza; answer the questions I shall ask.' (Bahira used these words because he had heard the Quraysh swearing by these two idols.) It is said that the apostle of Allah replied, 'Do not ask me by al-Lat and by al-Uzza; for, by Allah, I have never hated anything more intensely than these two.' Bahira continued, 'Then I adjure you by Allah to answer what I shall ask', and the apostle of Allah said, 'Ask me what thou wilt.' Accordingly he put to him various questions about his state during sleep, and his condition and circumstances, to which the apostle of Allah gave

THE LIFE OF MUHAMMAD

replies which agreed with what Bahira expected of him. Then Bahira looked on his back and discovered the seal of prophecy between his shoulders.

After he had examined the boy, Bahira went to Abu Talib and asked, 'What is this boy to you?' He replied, 'My son!' Bahira rejoined, 'He is not your son, nor is there any need for this boy to have a father living.' Abu Talib said, 'He is the son of my brother', and Bahira asked, 'What has become of his father?' When Abu Talib replied, 'He died whilst the boy's mother was pregnant with him', Bahira said, 'You have spoken the truth. Return with your nephew to his country, and guard him from the Jews; for, by Allah, if they see him and know about him what I know, they will try to injure him, because something very great will happen to this nephew of yours. Therefore make haste to return with him to his country.' Accordingly his uncle departed quickly with the apostle of Allah and took him to Mecca as soon as he had finished his trading in Syria.

According to the legend current among the people, three Christians or Jews named Zurayr, Tammam, and Daris, had the same information about the apostle of Allah as Bahira had. When they saw the boy during this same journey with his uncle Abu Talib, and contemplated doing him some harm, Bahira warned them against it and reminded them of God and of the description they would find in the scriptures; he said, too, that even if they persisted in their intention they could not carry it out. At last they understood and believed what he said, and they departed.

The apostle of Allah grew – Allah protecting, keeping and guarding him from the abominations of idolatry, having pre-destined him to become His apostle and the recipient of His grace – till he became the most excellent man of his people, the most agreeable in behaviour, the most noble in descent, the finest in neighbourly feeling, the greatest in meekness, and the most truthful in utterance; the greatest in fidelity, the furthest from wickedness and from acts which pollute; so exalted and noble that he was called among his people 'the faithful', because of the good qualities Allah had bestowed upon him.

The apostle of Allah later told how Allah had preserved him

in his childhood and state of innocence, saying, 'I was among Quraysh boys and we were carrying stones for some play. We were all naked, and every boy had placed his *ezar* [loincloth] round his neck to carry stones in it, and I had done the same as they. When I was thus moving about, some Being whom I did not see struck me a fearful blow and exclaimed, "Bind on thy *ezar*"; accordingly I girded myself therewith, and thus carried the stones on my neck, I being the only one among my companions who wore his *ezar*.'

The War of the Wicked broke out when the apostle of Allah was twenty years old, and it was called Wicked because during the sacred month two tribes, the Kinana and the Qays Aylan, considered it right to do what was not right at such a time. The Quraysh, after the sacred month, went to the aid of their allies, the Kinana. The apostle of Allah was taken out by his uncles during one battle to witness the fight, and he afterwards said, 'I was arrowing to my uncles, that is to say, I brought them the arrows, which the enemies had shot against them.'

When the apostle of Allah was twenty-five years old he married Khadija, a rich and noble merchant-woman who engaged men to sell her merchandise and allowed them part of the profits; the Quraysh was a trading tribe. She had heard of the veracity, honesty, and excellence of the apostle of Allah, and sent for him to propose that he take some of her goods to Syria as a trader. She promised to allow him a larger profit than other merchants, and to send with him her male slave, Maysara. The apostle of Allah accepted the offer and departed with the goods and the slave.

On his arrival in Syria the apostle of Allah alighted in the shade of a tree near the hermitage of a monk, who approached Maysara and asked, 'Who is this man under the tree?' Maysara replied, 'This man is one of the Quraysh from the sacred city.' And the monk said, 'Under this tree no one ever alighted except a prophet.'

Then the apostle of Allah sold the goods he had, purchased others, and returned with Maysara to Mecca. It is said that

Maysara saw, at noon during this return journey when the heat was strong, two angels shading the apostle of Allah from the sun while he rode on his camel. When he arrived at Mecca and came to Khadija with his goods, she sold them and found their value doubled or almost so. Maysara, too, informed her of what the monk had said, and what he had seen of the two angels shading the apostle; and Khadija – who was an intelligent, noble and good woman, predestined to great favour by Allah – sent for the apostle of Allah and spoke the following words: 'O son of my uncle! I have taken a liking to you on account of our relationship, your respectability among the people, your honesty, character and veracity.' Then she offered herself to him for a wife. She was at that time the most honoured woman among the Quraysh because of her lineage, the highest in nobility, and the richest in property; for this everybody envied her. When she had made this proposal to the apostle of Allah he mentioned it to his uncles, and his uncle, Hamza, went with him to her father, whom he asked for her; and he married her. The apostle of Allah gave her twenty young camels for a dowry. She was the first wife he married, and he never married another until she died.

Khadija bore to the apostle of Allah all his children except Ibrahim. She gave birth to al-Qasim, and to al-Tayyib, to al-Tahir, to Ruqayya, to Zaynab, to Umm Kulthum and to Fatima. Al-Qasim, al-Tayyib and al-Tahir died during 'ignorance' [before the promulgation of Islam], but all the daughters of the apostle of Allah lived to see the establishment of Islam, made profession of it, and emigrated with him to Medina.

Khadija told her cousin, Waraqa, who was a Christian well versed in sacred and profane literature, what Maysara had related of the conversation of the monk and what he had seen of the two angels shading the apostle of Allah, and Waraqa replied, 'If this be true, o Khadija, then Muhammad is the prophet of his people. I know that a prophet is expected at this time.'

Waraqa had been one of the men of the Quraysh known as the 'four inquirers', who had gone in search of the true religion of Abraham. This happened in the following manner:

THE FOUR INQUIRERS

Some decades earlier the Quraysh had begun to establish the rule of 'The Hums', which imposed acceptance of Quraysh superiority over the other Arab tribes. 'We are the sons of Abraham, men of honour, governors of the house of Allah, inhabitants of Mecca. No Arab has such virtue as we, nor such dignity as we. No man of the Quraysh should honour territory which is secular in the way he honours that which is sacred. For if he does so the Arabs will slight his honour, and will say of the Quraysh, "They have honoured that which is profane [outside the sacred limits] in the same way as that which is sacred [within the sanctuary of the holy territory of Mecca]." ' Accordingly the Quraysh abandoned certain holy ordinances of pilgrimage enjoined by the religion of Abraham, saying: 'We are the inhabitants of the sacred city of Mecca and it is not proper for us to leave it and honour another place as we honour Mecca. We are the Hums, the people of the sacred place.' But they imposed the ordinances on all other Arabs born either without or within the limits of Mecca.

They next invented new observances for themselves. They announced that it was not proper for the Hums to prepare *eqth* [milk to be dried and reduced to powder], to melt fat, or to enter a camel-hair tent whilst they were in a state of purity and sanctity [performing the ceremonies of the pilgrimage]. They added even to these rules, saying that persons who had come from outside the sacred city ought not to eat food they had brought in with them, whether they came as pilgrims or visitors. The pilgrims' first circuit of the Kaba should be made in dress provided by the Hums, or, if such could not be procured, in no dress at all; but rich men or women unwilling to do either could walk round the temple in the garments in which they had arrived, provided they afterwards threw them away and neither touched them any more nor allowed anyone else to touch them. The Arabs were induced to agree to this and made the circuit of the Kaba, the men naked, and the women clad only in an open cassock.

One day, when the Quraysh held a festival near one of the stone idols which they honoured, for which they slaughtered

sacrifices, near which they assiduously prayed, and around which
they walked in procession, four men (one of whom was Waraqa)
separated from the rest, saying one to another: 'Will we make a
covenant of mutual friendship and protection?' And each said,
'Indeed we will! Our people have no religion! They have lost
the religion of their father Abraham! What worth has a stone
that it should be walked around, which can neither hear nor see
anything, neither hurt nor profit anyone? O ye Quraysh, seek a
religion for yourself, for, by Allah, you have none whatever.'

And the four dispersed to various countries to seek the religion
of Abraham. Waraqa decided on Christianity and followed the
books of its teachers until he had obtained knowledge of the
scripture. Ubaydullah remained in doubt until, after the
revelation, he made profession of Islam and went to Abyssinia;
but when he arrived there he became a Christian and died thus,
after having renounced Islam.

The third, Uthman, went to Byzantium, where he became
a Christian and attained high office.

The fourth man, Zayd, became neither Jew nor Christian,
although he renounced the religion of the Quraysh and abandoned idols, blood, and sacrifices slain for idols, and condemned
the burying alive of female infants. He said, 'I worship the Lord
of Abraham', and, when he was a very old man, was to be seen
leaning with his back against the Kaba, saying, 'O ye Quraysh
people! I swear by Him in whose hand the life of Zayd is, there
is not one among you of the religion of Abraham, except myself.
O Allah! If I knew which way is most pleasing to Thee, I would
worship Thee according to it, but I do not know it.' He set forth
in search of the religion of Abraham and made inquiries from
monks and Jewish priests. He passed through Mesopotamia, and
then wandered through the whole of Syria until he found a
monk in whom the knowledge of Christianity was concentrated.
Him he asked about the orthodox religion of Abraham, and the
monk replied, 'You are in search of a religion to which no one
can guide you at present; but the time is at hand when a prophet
will arise in your country; he will be sent with the religion of
Abraham. Adopt it, for he comes now, and this is the time.'

Shortly after this Zayd departed for Mecca, but he was attacked and died by the way.

When the apostle of Allah was thirty-five years old some evil men stole the treasure which was kept in a well inside the Kaba. The treasure was found again in the possession of a manumitted slave, and the Quraysh cut off his hands, although they believed that others had stolen the treasure and merely left it with the slave.

The Quraysh now felt it necessary to rebuild the Kaba and to roof it in, but they were afraid to demolish it, because there was a serpent which always came up to the wall to warm itself. The people feared it because when anyone approached it raised itself, hissed and opened its mouth. One day, however, whilst it was warming itself as usual in the sun on the wall, Allah sent a bird which snatched it up and flew off with it. Thereon the Quraysh said: 'Allah must approve of our intention. We have a workman, we possess wood, and Allah has delivered us from the serpent.'

They were now firmly determined to pull down the Kaba and to build it up again, and Abu Wahb rose and took a stone from the Kaba. But the stone leapt from his hand and returned to its place, and he exclaimed: 'O ye Quraysh people! In the building of the Kaba, do not employ any of your goods unless they be of righteous origin; do not use in it the profit of iniquity, nor of usurious sale, nor of injustice towards any man.'

The Quraysh had decided that different parts of the Kaba should be demolished by different sections of the community, but the people were still afraid to destroy the edifice. Then al-Walid said: 'I shall make a beginning for you', and he took up a pickaxe, stood up before the Kaba and declared: 'O Allah! Let us not be afraid! We want only what is good!' Then he began to pull down the wall between the two buttresses. But the people waited that night, saying: 'We shall see; and if anything happens to al-Walid, we shall not demolish it, but leave it as it was; but if nothing befalls him, Allah is pleased with what we have done for its demolition.' The next morning al-Walid continued his work of demolition, and the people aided him till they reached the foundations. In the buttress they found an inscription in Syriac, and knew not what it meant until a Jew read it for them. It was as follows: 'I am Allah, the lord of Mecca! I created it when I created the heavens and the earth, when I fashioned the sun and the moon, and I have appointed over it seven angels; Mecca will not perish until its two hills perish! It will be blessed to its inhabitants in water and milk!' When they reached the foundations they found them to be green boulders adhering together like a single stone, and when a man of the Quraysh inserted a lever to separate the boulders, the whole of Mecca began to shake; so the people touched the foundation no more.

The groups of Quraysh now collected stones for the re-building, each group gathering separately, and they built until they reached the spot for the *ruku* [the sacred black stone]. Then all the people quarrelled, because each group wished the honour of lifting the stone into place; so bitter were the quarrels that the groups made alliances and prepared to fight. One group pro-duced a dish filled with blood and entered into a covenant unto death with another group by dipping their hands into the dish; they were therefore called blood-lickers. The situation remained thus for four or five nights; then the Quraysh assembled in the mosque to consult and reach a decision, and the oldest man among them said at last, 'Why not let he who next enters through the door of this mosque be the arbiter in this quarrel, and let him decide it?' They agreed, and the first man who entered was the apostle of Allah. And they said, 'This is the faithful one! We agree that he shall judge.' When he came near they told him of the problem and he said, 'Bring me a cloak'. When they had brought one, he placed the *ruku* [black stone] in it with his own hands, saying, 'Let every group take hold of a part of the cloak.' Then all of them lifted it together, and when they reached the spot, the apostle placed it in position with his own hands, and the building was continued over it.

Thus matters stood when Allah sent for Muhammad, His pro-phet, and revealed to him His religion and the proper usages of the pilgrimage. 'Therefore go [ye Quraysh] in procession as the people [the other Arabs] go in procession, and ask pardon from Allah; because Allah is forgiving and merciful.' As for the prohibitions invented by the Quraysh concerning cooking, dress, the circuit of the Kaba, and food brought from beyond the sacred territory, Allah revealed the following: 'O children of Adam! Wear decent apparel at every place of worship, and eat, and drink but be not prodigal, for He loveth not prodigals. Say, who has forbidden the decent apparel of Allah which He has brought forth for His servants, and the good things of His providing? Say, these benefits, especially on the day of resurrection, shall be for those who were believers during their present life.' Thus, when Allah established Islam by sending his apostle, he set aside the observances the Quraysh had invented for their people.

THE REVELATION

As the time approached for the revelation of the apostle, Jewish priests and Christian monks discussed prophecies concerning the event contained in their sacred books and inherited from their own prophets.

One day, according to an Arab tribesman, 'I was lying in the courtyard of our family house and a Jew who conducted business with us told us of the day of judgement, the resurrection, the reckoning, of paradise and of hell. We who were idolaters had no knowledge of the resurrection, and said, "Woe be unto you! Do you think it possible that men will be raised up after death in a place where there is a paradise and a hell, and in which they will be requited according to their acts?" And he assured us, by Him who is sworn by, that he would prefer to be cast into the greatest oven in this world, scorching though it might be and sealed tight, rather than face the torments of hell in the next. My kinsmen said, "What will be the sign?" and he replied, "A prophet will arise in the direction of this country", and pointed towards Mecca and Yemen. They asked, "When will this happen?" and, looking at me, the youngest of the people, he said, "When this boy's life attains maturity he will see him." And by

Allah, not a day nor a night passed after that until the time when Allah sent his apostle to live among us during which we did not expect his arrival. But when it came, that refractory and envious Jew refused to become a believer, even after the apostle had promulgated Islam, and we said, "Woe be to you! Did you not yourself inform us about the prophet?" And he replied, "Indeed! But not about this one!" '

There was also a Syrian Jew who paid a visit to the Banu Qurayza, a Jewish tribe, several years before the establishment of Islam and settled down among them; and many later said they had never seen a man who did not recite five prayers daily [i.e. who was not a Muslim] of a better character than he. He remained with them, and when they suffered from drought they said to him, 'Come, and procure us water!' After being paid with dates and barley, he went out into the fields and prayed to Allah for rain, and did not move until clouds came and drenched him. This he did not once, twice or thrice, but many times. As his death approached, he said, 'Why do you think I came away from the land of abundance to the land of misfortune and famine? I have come to this country to await the arrival of a prophet, whose time is near at hand; and it is to this country that he will flee. I hoped he would be sent during my lifetime, that I might follow him. His time is near at hand. Do not allow others to forestall you in believing in his mission; for he will be sent to shed the blood, and to capture the children and women, of those who oppose him; but let not this hinder you from following him.' Years later, when the apostle of Allah besieged the Banu Qurayza, the friends of the dead Jew said, 'By Allah! This is the prophet foretold to us. This is he according to his description!' They accordingly came down from their fort, made profession of Islam, and thus preserved their lives, their property and families.

Like the Jews and Christians, the Arab soothsayers also spoke of the coming of an apostle, but their people paid no heed until Allah actually sent him, when, the prophecies made by the soothsayers having been fulfilled, the people became aware of their significance. Whereas the Jews and Christians culled their

prophecies from scripture, the Arab soothsayers received their
foreknowledge of most events from the djinns, spirits of the air
who stole information by listening close to heaven. But when the
coming of the apostle was close at hand meteors from heaven
were hurled at all the djinns and they were driven away from the
places where they used to sit and listen; and they realized that
this was by the command of Allah.

The first Arabs to be struck with fear at the sight of the shooting stars – for that was how the meteors thrown at the djinns
appeared on earth – went to the wisest man of their tribe and said,
'Have you seen what happened in the sky and the falling of some
of the stars?' He replied, 'If the stars thrown down were those
which serve as signs and guides by land and sea, those by which
the seasons of summer and winter are defined and by which the
various affairs of mankind are regulated, then by Allah the world
has come to an end with all the people thereof; but if those stars
remain in their places and it is others which have been hurled
down, then Allah has a different intention and does not mean to
destroy creation.'

Afterwards, the apostle of Allah asked some men of Medina
what had been said there about the falling stars and was told:
'We said, "A king has died or has begun to reign; a child has
been born, or has died." ' The apostle of Allah replied: 'It was
not so. When Allah reaches any decision concerning His people
He is heard by the bearers of His throne, who praise Him; and
this praise is taken up by the angels below them, and by others
still further below; and the praise continues to descend until it
reaches the sky of this world, where other angels also praise.
Then these ask each other why they praise, and the question
ascends gradually till it reaches the bearers of the throne. They
then, tell of the decree of Allah concerning His people, and the
news travels down by degrees until it reaches the heaven of this
world, where the angels discuss it. But the evil djinns, who used
to listen to such discussions by stealth, sometimes misheard, and
what they retailed to soothsayers on earth was sometimes true
and sometimes false. The soothsayers also conversed about these
matters, some giving true and some false accounts. So, when the

coming of the apostle was being discussed by the angels, Allah foiled the evil djinns by hurling meteors, and from that time onwards an end was made to soothsayers.'

For some time the mind of Muhammad had been in a state of religious ferment. The religious aspect, however, was not without political overtones, as can be seen in the parts of the Koran dating from this period: and an imperfect understanding of Christianity and Judaism coloured the beginnings (and, indeed, the later development) of the new religion in his mind. At the start of his mission, Muhammad saw himself as the latest in the line of prophets which began with Moses and ended with Jesus of Nazareth.

When Muhammad was forty years old Allah sent him as a prophet of mercy to the people of the visible and of the invisible worlds, and to all mankind.

With every prophet whom Allah had sent before the time of Muhammad, He had made a covenant, binding each of them to believe in the coming of Muhammad, to declare him a true apostle, to aid him against every opponent, and to testify to every man who believed in the truth of their own prophetic missions that the mission of Muhammad was still to come. They complied, according to His command, and spread the covenant of Allah to all who believed in them, so that many men who believed in the Old or the New Testament believed also in the truth of this covenant.

According to his wife, the first prophetic sign shown by the apostle of Allah – after Allah determined to honour him and, through him, to show mercy to His servants – took the form of true visions. That is to say, the apostle of Allah never had a vision in his sleep; instead, it came like the break of day. She also said that Allah made him love solitude, so that he loved nothing more than to be alone.

When Allah had determined on the coming of the apostle of Allah, Muhammad went out on some business at such a distance that he left human habitation behind and came to deep valleys. He did not pass by a stone or a tree but it said 'Salutation to thee, o apostle of Allah!' The apostle turned to his right, to his left, and looked behind, but saw nothing except trees and stones. Thus he remained for some time looking and listening, till Gabriel came to him with that revelation which the grace of Allah was to bestow upon him when he was at Hira during the month of Ramadan.

Every year the apostle of Allah spent a month praying at Hira and fed the poor who came to him; and when he returned to Mecca he walked round the Kaba seven or more times, as it pleased Allah, before entering his own house. In the month of Ramadan, in the year when Allah designed to bestow grace upon him, the apostle of Allah went to Hira as usual, and his family accompanied him. In the night the angel Gabriel came with the command of Allah. The apostle of Allah later said, 'He came while I was asleep, with a cloth of brocade whereon there was writing, and he said, "Read." I replied, "I cannot read it." Then he pressed the cloth on me till I thought I was dying; he released his hold and said, "Read." I replied, "I cannot read it." And he pressed me again with it, till I thought I was dying. Then he loosed his hold of me and said, "Read." I replied, "I cannot read it." Once more he pressed me and said, "Read." Then I asked, "What shall I read?" And I said this because I feared he would press me again. Then he said, "Read in the name of the Lord thy creator; who created man from a drop of blood. Read, thy Lord is the most bountiful, who taught by means of the pen, taught man what he knew not." Accordingly I read these words, and he had finished his task and departed from me. I awoke from my sleep, and felt as if words had been graven on my heart.'

This reading is, in fact, recorded in the Koran. From this point on in the text, every revelation from Allah appears in the wording of a Sura (chapter) or verse in the Koran, the Muslim bible which is neither more nor less than a compilation of the revelations vouchsafed by Allah to Muhammad. Appearing here as they do in the context of the events to which they refer, these revelations are – in spite of their inspirational overtones – a logical reflection of what was happening at the time.

'Afterwards I went out, and when I was on the centre of the mountain, I heard a voice from heaven, saying, "O Muhammad! Thou art the prophet of Allah, and I am Gabriel." I raised my head to look at the sky, and lo! I beheld Gabriel in the shape of a man with extended wings, standing in the firmament, with his feet touching the ground. And he said again, "O Muhammad! Thou art the apostle of Allah, and I am Gabriel." I continued to gaze at him, neither advancing nor retreating. Then I turned my face away from him to other parts of the sky, but in whatever direction I looked I saw him in the same form. I remained thus, neither advancing nor retreating, and Khadija sent messengers to search for me. They went as far as the highest part of Mecca and again returned to her, while I remained standing on the same spot, until the angel departed from me and I returned to my family.

'When I came to Khadija I narrated to her what I had seen, and she said, "Be of good cheer and comfort thyself! I swear by Him in whose hand the life of Khadija is, that I hope thou wilt be the prophet of this nation!" Then she rose, collected her garments around her and departed to Waraqa.' She described to him what the apostle of Allah had seen and heard, and Waraqa exclaimed, 'Holy! Holy! I swear to Him in whose hands the life of Waraqa is that the law of Moses has been bestowed on him and he is the prophet of this nation! Tell him to stand firm.' Khadija then returned to the apostle of Allah and informed him of what Waraqa had said.

When the apostle of Allah ended his sojourn at Hira he departed to Mecca and went first round the Kaba as was his habit. And he was met by Waraqa, who said, 'Thou wilt be accused of falsehood, thou wilt be persecuted, exiled, and attacked.' Then Waraqa bent his head towards the apostle and kissed him on the crown of the head, and the apostle of Allah departed to his house.

But the revelations were not continued and the apostle became much downcast, until Gabriel came to him with a message from Allah saying that He had not abandoned Muhammad; 'By brightness, and by the night when it is dark, thy Lord has not forsaken nor hated thee, and the next life will be better for thee than the first. The Lord will give thee victory in this world and reward in the next. Did He not find thee an orphan and procure thee shelter? He found thee erring and guided thee; He found thee needy and enriched thee.' The message to Muhammad continued: 'Declare the goodness of thy Lord; declare what has come to thee from Allah, and declare His bounty and grace in thy mission; mention it, record it, and pray for manifestations of it.' Accordingly the apostle of Allah began, at first in secret to those of his family whom he trusted, to promulgate the gospel bestowed by Allah on him, and on mankind through his agency.

Prayer was made an ordinance to Muhammad, and accordingly he prayed. The apostle of Allah was first commanded to make two prayer-flexions [prostrations] for every prayer, but later Allah commanded four prayer-flexions for those who were at home, although He confirmed the first ordinance of two prayer-flexions for those who were on a journey.

When prayer was made obligatory to the apostle of Allah, Gabriel came to him when he was in the highest part of Mecca, and spurred his heel into the ground towards the valley; a spring gushed forth and Gabriel performed religious ablutions. The apostle of Allah observed how purification for prayers was to be made, and washed himself likewise. Then Gabriel rose and prayed, and the apostle of Allah did so after him, and then Gabriel departed. When the apostle of Allah came to Khadija he performed the religious ablution in her presence to show her how purity was attained, just as Gabriel had done. And she, too, washed as she had been shown. Then the apostle prayed as Gabriel had prayed, and Khadija prayed after him.

Then Gabriel came to him and held noon-prayers when the sun passed the zenith; and prayed the afternoon prayers with him when his shadow was the same length as his own body. Then he prayed the sunset prayers when the sun disappeared, and the last evening prayer when the twilight disappeared. Next day he held morning prayers with the apostle at dawn; then the midday prayers when the shadow was one with him; and the afternoon prayers when it was twice as long as he; then the sunset orisons when the sun disappeared, as on the preceding day. Then he prayed with him the last evening prayers when the first third of the night had elapsed, and lastly the morning prayers, when the morning dawned but the sun had not yet risen. Then he said, 'O Muhammad! The time of prayer is between thy prayers of yesterday and today.'

The first man to believe in the apostle of Allah, to pray with him and accept his prophetic mission, was Ali, who at that time was ten years old. Even before Islam, Allah had favoured him by allowing him to live under the protection of the apostle of Allah. The Quraysh had been visited by severe famine, and, as Abu Talib had a numerous family, the apostle of Allah went to another uncle, al-Abbas – who was among the wealthiest of the tribe – and said, 'Your brother Abu Talib has a large family and you must be aware from what scarcity the people are suffering. Come therefore with me, and we shall ease him of his burden. I shall take one of his sons, and do you take another under your care.' Al-Abbas agreed, and they went to Abu Talib and said, 'We wish to alleviate your troubles until the people are released from their distress.' Accordingly, the apostle of Allah took Ali and pressed him to his heart, and al-Abbas took Jafar.

Ali remained with the apostle of Allah and followed him, believed in him, and accepted the truth of his doctrines. When the time of prayer was at hand, the apostle of Allah habitually went out to the valleys of Mecca, and took Ali with him, unknown to his father Abu Talib or to his people; and they prayed together and returned in the evening. This continued for some time, until one day Abu Talib happened to discover them at prayer and asked the apostle of Allah, 'What religion is this I see you practising?' He replied, 'This is the religion of Allah, and of His angels, of His apostles, and of our father Abraham. Allah has sent me with this religion, as an apostle to His servants; and you, my uncle, are the most worthy on whom I could bestow advice and invitation to guidance; you are the most worthy to comply in it and to aid me therein.' But Abu Talib said, 'I cannot abandon the religion of my forefathers and what they believed in; but no harm shall be done to you as long as I live.' It is also said that he asked Ali, 'What religion is this thou believest in?' and Ali replied, 'I believe in the apostle of Allah, and that his revelation is true. I pray with him, and I follow him.' His father said, 'He has called thee only to what is good; therefore obey him.'

Next, Zayd, the manumitted slave of the apostle of Allah, made his profession of Islam, being the second man who did so. The youth Zayd had arrived from Syria as a slave, and the nephew of Khadija said to her, 'Select any of these slaves you wish, as a present.' She chose Zayd and took him away, but when the apostle saw him he asked for him. Khadija agreed, and the apostle of Allah gave him his liberty and adopted him as his son. (This was before the apostle had received the revelation.) Meanwhile, the father of Zayd mourned for him and wept for his loss; but at last he found his son with the apostle of Allah. The apostle said to Zayd, 'Remain with me if you wish, or depart with your father if you wish', and Zayd replied, 'I shall abide with you!' Accordingly he never parted from the apostle until Allah bestowed his mission on him. Zayd then professed Islam.

Next Abu Bakr, called *Assidiq* ('The True'), made his profession of Islam, confessing it publicly. The apostle of Allah later said, 'I have preached Islam to no one who did not hesitate, consider, and contradict, save Abu Bakr, who neither hesitated nor was perplexed.' Abu Bakr invited the people to believe in Allah the most high and glorious, and in His apostle. He was popular with his people, amiable, and compassionate, and was unusually well acquainted with Quraysh genealogy, and with whatever was good or evil therein. He was a merchant, of humane and kindly disposition, so that the people of his tribe sought after his company more than that of any other man, on account of his knowledge, his scrupulous honesty, and his friendly conversation. He now invited to Islam all the people who trusted in him, and associated with him.

At his invitation Uthman made profession of Islam, as well as al-Zubayr, Abdul-Rahman, Sad b. Abu Waqqas, and Talha. Abu Bakr went with them to the apostle of Allah and they made their profession of Islam and prayed. These eight men preceded all others in Islam; they prayed, they believed in the apostle of

Allah, and accepted as true the revelation which had come to him from Allah.

Soon several men and women had made their profession of Islam and it was much discussed in Mecca. Then Allah commanded his apostle to make public the revelation and to invite the people to accept it; hitherto, for the three years since his first revelation, it had been kept secret by the apostle. Allah said to him, 'Publish that which thou hast been commanded, and turn away from the idolaters.'

When the apostle began to spread Islam among his people as Allah had commanded him, they did not gainsay him until he began to abuse their idols; but when he had done this, they accused him of seeking power, denied his revelation, and united to injure him. The companions of the apostle of Allah went into the valleys to pray, unknown to the people; and once, whilst Sad and several companions of the apostle were at prayer, they were discovered by idolaters who heaped insults upon them, condemned their deeds, and provoked them to fight. Then Sad struck an idolater with the jawbone of a camel, and wounded him; and this was the first blood shed in Islam.

But Abu Talib, uncle of the apostle, defended him. Several nobles of the Quraysh, including Utba and Abu Sufyan, went to Abu Talib and said, 'Your nephew has insulted our gods and condemned our religion. He considers our young men to be fools, and our fathers to have erred. You must either restrain him or allow us free action against him, since your religion is the same as ours, opposed to his.' But the apostle continued to preach the religion of Allah and to seek conversions, and the people hated him. Again they went to Abu Talib and said, 'You are aged, noble, and highly respected among us, and we have already asked you to prohibit your nephew from offending us. But you have not prohibited him, and, by Allah, we shall not overlook his insults unless you guarantee his future good behaviour. Otherwise, we shall fight both him and you.' After this they departed, and Abu Talib was much grieved by the enmity of his tribe; but he could not surrender or desert the apostle of Allah.

After this visit, Abu Talib sent for the apostle and said, 'Consider my life and yours, and do not burden me with what I cannot bear.' The apostle of Allah feared from these words that his uncle, being too weak, had determined to desert him and he replied, 'If they were to place the sun in my right and the moon in my left hand, I would not abandon my mission.' Then tears started in his eyes and he wept. But when he turned to depart Abu Talib said, 'Nephew! Go, and speak what you wish. By Allah! I shall never fail you.'

And the nobles went once more to Abu Talib and offered him the brilliant youth Umara in exchange for Muhammad, but he replied, 'It is a wicked thing you propose, that you give me your son to feed, and I give you mine to kill! This shall never be.'

Then the Quraysh incited each other to enmity towards the companions of the apostle of Allah, and persecuted them, and endeavoured to lead them astray from their religion. But Allah protected His apostle and Abu Talib, and Abu Talib gathered his friends around him.

When the season of pilgrimage was at hand, the Quraysh assembled to agree on the attitude they should display about the apostle. They asked, 'Shall we call him a soothsayer?' but al-Walid, the chief, replied, 'He is not a soothsayer. We have seen soothsayers; he does not murmur and rhyme as they do.' They continued, 'Then we shall say that he is possessed by djinns.' He replied, 'He is not possessed. We have seen lunatics and know them. He does not gasp, nor roll his eyes, nor mutter.' They said, 'Then we shall say that he is a poet.' Al-Walid replied, 'He is not a poet. We know all the poets and their styles. He is not a poet.' They asked, 'Then what shall we say?' Al-Walid replied, 'You cannot say any of these things, for it will be known that they are false. The best will be to say that he is a sorcerer, because he has come with words which are sorcery and which separate a man from his father or from his brother, or from his wife, or from his family.'

When the season of the pilgrimage arrived, the Quraysh sat by the roadside and allowed no man to pass without warning

him about Muhammad. And the Arab pilgrims carried away
from Mecca news of the apostle of Allah, so that his fame spread
over the whole country.

When Islam began to spread in Mecca, the Quraysh imprisoned
its believers or sought to turn them away from Islam. The
nobles sent for Muhammad in order to justify themselves, and
the apostle of Allah hastened to them in the hope that they had
conceived a favourable opinion of what he had told them. But
they only accused him once more of seeking riches and power.
This he denied, and reaffirmed his mission from Allah. Then they
said, 'You know that no people are in greater want of land, of
water and of food than we are. Ask the Lord who has sent you
to take away these mountains which confine us and to level out
the country, to cause rivers to gush forth like the rivers of Syria,
and to resurrect our ancestors that we may ask them whether
what you say is true or false. If they declare you to be truthful
and if you do what we have asked, we shall believe you and shall
know that Allah has sent you to be an apostle.' He replied, 'I
have not been sent to you with this, but I have brought to you
from Allah the revelation He has sent. If you reject it, I appeal in
this affair to Allah, that He decide between me and you.'

They continued, 'Ask, then, your Lord to send an angel to
bear witness to your veracity. Ask Him to give you gardens,
palaces and treasures of gold and silver to enrich you; we know
you go now to the markets to procure food as we procure it. Then
we shall know your rank and station with Allah.' The apostle of
Allah said, 'I shall not do this, nor ask for this. I was not sent to
you for this; but Allah has sent me as a bearer of glad tidings and
a preacher.'

They went on, 'Then cause the heavens to fall upon us, for
we shall not believe you unless you do something miraculous.'
The apostle of Allah replied, 'This is the choice of Allah! If He
wishes, He will do it.' Then they said, 'We shall not cease to
persecute you until we destroy you or you destroy us. We shall
not believe you until you come with Allah and all the angels.'

So the apostle of Allah returned home, sad and downcast with

THE LIFE OF MUHAMMAD

disappointment in his people and their estrangement from him.

When the apostle had left them, Abu Jahl said, 'I now make a vow to Allah, that I shall wait for him tomorrow with a stone as large as I can carry and when he prostrates himself in prayer, I shall smash his head with it! After that you may either surrender me or defend me.' They replied, 'We shall never surrender you!' Next morning, Abu Jahl took a stone as he had said, and waited for the apostle of Allah, who arrived and prayed as usual at Mecca with his face towards the Kaba and Syria beyond. Abu Jahl approached him; but suddenly he turned back and fled, his countenance altered, so frightened that his hands could not hold the stone. 'When I approached,' he said, 'a stallion-camel appeared before me with a skull, a collar bone, and teeth the like of which I have never seen. It rushed to devour me.'

Later, Utba, who was a prince among the Quraysh, said, 'Shall I speak to Muhammad so that he may cease to trouble us?' They said, 'Yes, go and speak to him.' So Utba went to Muhammad, and said, 'You have disturbed our concord; listen to my proposal and consider it, that you may perchance accept a part thereof. If property be your desire in this affair, we shall collect as much of it as will make you the richest of us; but if dignity be your object, we shall make you our prince so that no affair will be decided without you; and if you want to be a king, we shall make you our king; but if this be a spirit who visits you and you are unable to repel it, we shall find a physician for you and give him money till he cures you of it.' The apostle of Allah listened and then recited to him a verse from the Koran, and Utba returned to his companions, saying, 'I have heard words the like of which I have never heard. This is neither poetry, nor sorcery, nor soothsaying. Do not interfere with this man or his vocation but let him alone. The words which I have heard will spread far and wide. If others should kill him, you will be rid of him, but if he conquers the Arabs, then his power will be your power, and his glory your glory, so that you will through him become the happiest of people.' But they thought him bewitched.

After this, the Quraysh sent al-Nadr, a bitter enemy of Muhammad, and Uqba to the Jewish priests in Medina with instructions to ask about the apostle, for they said the Jews 'are the possessors of the first book [the Pentateuch] and have knowledge about prophets which we have not'. The Jewish priests told them, 'Ask him three questions which we shall give you. If he answers them obey him, for he is a prophet; but if not, then he is a pretender, and you may deal with him as you think proper.'

Al-Nadr and Uqba returned to Mecca and told the people what the priests had said, and they said to the apostle, 'Inform us about the young men who passed away in ancient times, because their case is wonderful; tell us also about the traveller who went from the east to the west of the earth, and tell us about the soul and what it is!' The apostle of Allah replied: 'I shall tell you tomorrow.'

Two weeks, however, passed and the apostle received no revelation from Allah and no visit from Gabriel, and the people of Mecca began to murmur against him. At last Gabriel came and the apostle of Allah said, 'Thou hast remained away from me so long that I became troubled by evil imaginings!' Gabriel replied, 'We descend only by command of thy Lord! To Him belongs the present, the past, and whatever is between them. Nor is thy Lord ever forgetful.' And Gabriel brought a revelation from Allah in the form of the Sura known as *The Cave*. Part of the revelation contained a warning that 'We will surely reduce whatever is on earth to dust and desolation. To Me you must return, and I shall requite everyone according to his works; do not therefore be distressed or grieved about what thou seest or hearest on earth.'

Then Gabriel told the apostle the answer concerning the young men whose case was wonderful. 'Verily they were young men who believed in the Lord and We increased our guidance to them, and We fortified their hearts, and they said "Our Lord is the Lord of heaven and earth, we shall invoke no other god besides him, for that would be to utter sacrilege." And they took refuge in a cave from those who worshipped idols; and thou mightest have seen the sun, when it rose, pass from their cave to the right, and when it went down it left them on the left hand,

and they were in the centre thereof. This is one of the signs of
Allah that will satisfy thy questioners. An onlooker would have
thought the youths to be awake, though they were sleeping; and
their rulers said, "We shall build a place of worship over
them."'

'And the men dwelt in their cave three hundred years, and
nine more. Say, "Allah knows best how long they remained. He
possesses the secret of the heavens and of the earth. How well
He sees and hears! They have no other master besides Him, and
He makes no one His associate in judgment."'

Gabriel continued by warning Muhammad: 'Say not of anything "I shall do this tomorrow", without adding "If Allah
willeth it". Namely, never say as thou hast done in this instance
"I shall inform you tomorrow", but reserve the will of Allah.
Remember thy Lord if thou knowest not an answer, and say
"Perhaps my Lord will guide me to the information about which
you have asked". Thou knowest not what Allah will decide.

Then Gabriel told the apostle of Dhul-Qarnayn [possibly
another name for Alexander the Great], the traveller who was
gifted like no other man, and to whom the roads were opened so
that he travelled to the east and the west, even to a place where
the people scarcely understood the sound of the voice, and he
built a rampart faced with molten brass.

'They will ask thee also about the spirit. Say "The spirit
stems from the command of my Lord, and as to knowledge, ye
have yet received but little of it."'

When the apostle of Allah gave the people these replies, they
were convinced of the truth of his position as a prophet, but envy
prevented them from following him, and they continued in their
unbelief, attempting to mock the apostle because they feared
they would be defeated in honest argument.

Whenever the apostle of Allah recited the Koran aloud in his
devotions, they refused to listen to him, save some who approached secretly and stayed only as long as they were not observed by the Quraysh. The injunction from Allah, 'Do not
utter thy prayers too loud nor too low, but keep a balance between
them' was given the apostle because of such men; prayer must

not be too loud, or the people would go away; and not too low, lest he who listened by stealth and who might in some measure profit by it, would not be able to hear.

On a certain occasion, however, when the companions of the apostle of Allah were assembled, they said, 'The Quraysh have never heard this Koran publicly spoken. Who is the man who will let them hear it?' Abdullah replied, 'I will!' but they said, 'We fear they will injure you. It should be a man whose people can defend him against the tribe.' Abdullah insisted, 'Let me do it! Allah will protect me!' Accordingly, he made his appearance next morning at daylight, and spoke: 'In the name of Allah the merciful, the compassionate! The merciful who taught the Koran.' The Quraysh asked, 'What says that son of a slave-woman?' Then they leapt up and belaboured him, but he continued to recite as much of the Koran as Allah willed, and afterwards returned to his companions. 'The enemies of Allah never seemed to me to be more despicable than now,' he said. 'If you wish, I shall serve them in the same way tomorrow!' But they said, 'Let it suffice! You have caused them to hear what they dislike.'

The followers of Muhammad were often subjected to torture and some gave up their belief through weakness, some because of their great sufferings; but others were protected and strengthened by Allah so that they remained steadfast.

Bilal, a slave to one of the Banu Jumah, was of a pure heart and sincere in his profession of Islam. He was dragged out by Ummaya when the midday sun was hot and thrown on his back out in the valley of Mecca. A great stone was placed on his breast, and he was told, 'Remain thus until you expire, or until you renounce Muhammad and worship al-Lat and al-Uzza.' But during all this pain he merely repeated, 'One God! One!' Abu Bakr, chancing to pass by on a day when Bilal was suffering thus, said to his torturer, Ummaya, 'Do you not fear Allah?' but he replied, 'You have corrupted the slave! You can pull him out from under his burden!' Abu Bakr said, 'I shall do so; I have a black boy, smarter and stronger in your faith than this; I shall give him to you in exchange.' Accordingly Abu Bakr gave

Ummaya his slave and took Bilal, whom he presented with his freedom, as he did six other slaves who professed Islam.

The idolaters so tormented many companions of the apostle of Allah that their apostasy from Islam was excusable. They used to beat a man and to make him suffer hunger and thirst until he was unable to sit upright, such was his agony, and he would finally succumb to temptation and agree to all they asked of him. They would say to him, 'Al-Lat and al-Uzza are your gods as well as Allah', and he would agree. They went so far that, when even a dung-beetle happened to crawl by, they exclaimed, 'This is your god!' and he would agree in order to be rid of them and of his pain.

When the apostle of Allah saw the distress which his companions suffered, while he himself enjoyed comparative immunity under the protection of Allah and of his uncle Abu Talib, and that he was unable to save them, he said, 'If you were to go to the country of the Abyssinians, you would do well; there is a king there under whom no one is persecuted; it is a country of truth where you can remain until Allah grants you deliverance from the miseries of the present.' So the companions of the apostle of Allah emigrated for fear of temptation, flying for refuge, and those who emigrated were eighty-three in number. Among them was Ubaydullah, one of the 'four inquirers'.

These and similar events had occurred over a period of several years, the Quraysh becoming progressively more bitter about Muhammad. The apostle himself had too much moral protection from such elders as Abu Talib to suffer more than unpleasantness at their hands; there was little physical violence, and his attackers confined themselves mainly to slander and sneers.

The Quraysh now sent a deputation to the Negus of Abyssinia, asking for the return of the fugitives ('the first emigrants'), but the Negus chose to shelter them. Meanwhile, at Mecca, the faith continued to spread.

Rukana, the strongest of the Quraysh in physical power, happened one day to be with Muhammad in one of the passes, and the latter addressed him thus, 'Will you not fear Allah, and accept the revelation which I offer you?' He replied, 'If I knew what you say to be true, I would follow you!' The apostle of Allah asked, 'Will you know my statements to be true if I prostrate you to the ground?' Rukana said, 'Yes', and the apostle continued, 'Then rise that I may throw you down.' Accordingly Rukana rose to the attack, but as soon as the apostle of Allah assailed him, he fell to the ground helpless. After a while, he said, 'Once more, o Muhammad!' But he was knocked down again. And the apostle of Allah said, 'I shall show you something more wonderful still, if you will promise to fear Allah and to follow my religion. I shall call out to this tree here and it will come to me.' Accordingly he called it, and it approached till it stood fast before the apostle of Allah; then he said to the tree, 'Return to thy place!' and it returned to its place.

While the apostle of Allah was at Mecca twenty or so Christians arrived to visit him from Abyssinia, having heard of his fame. They found him in the mosque, and sat down with him and conversed and asked questions. After they had asked their questions, and been answered, the apostle of Allah invited them to become believers in Allah the most high and glorious, and recited to them the Koran. As they listened, tears flowed from their eyes and they believed in him and in his truth.

One day a slave girl saw Abu Jahl insult the apostle who made no reply; when, shortly afterwards, Hamza – a great hunter, who was also uncle and foster-brother of Muhammad – returned from the chase with his bow hanging from his shoulder, she told him of the event. Hamza was filled with great wrath – because Allah had predestined him for great favours – and hastened away to punish Abu Jahl. Approaching him, he struck him a fearful blow, saying, 'Dare you insult him, when I am of his religion and say what he says? Return my blow if you are able!' Several witnesses rose to aid Abu Jahl, but he exclaimed, 'Let Hamza alone, for I have insulted his nephew shamefully.' Hamza then completed his profession of Islam, begun in the haste of passion, by following the advice of the apostle in all the ordinances, and after this the Quraysh realized that Muhammad had even stronger protection and so ceased their worst incitements.

Another valuable convert at this time was Umar, hitherto a vociferous enemy of the apostle.

When the deputation of Quraysh returned disappointed from Abyssinia, the tribe decided to counteract Muhammad's influence by forming a league against him and his followers. They applied economic and social sanctions, forbade trade with him, and banned the Believers from marrying Quraysh women. This boycott had some success and the apostle lived almost in a state of siege for close on three years, except during the period of pilgrimage. All he could do was consolidate the faith of those who were with him. At last, however, the ban was lifted through the influence of several Quraysh who, though not Believers, sympathized with their plight. The apostle was now fifty years of age.

The apostle, by the orders of Allah, continued patiently, confidently, and lovingly to preach to his people, despite their accusations of falsehood, their insults, and their mockeries. The worst mockers were five in number, and after these men had persisted in their wickedness for some time, and had heaped their mockeries upon the apostle of Allah, the following verse was revealed: 'We shall suffice thee against the mockers who worship another god with Allah; they will know.'

Gabriel came to the apostle of Allah whilst these five were circumambulating the Kaba, and the apostle of Allah rose and stood by the side of Gabriel. When the first mocker passed by Gabriel threw a green leaf into his face, and he became blind. Then another passed to whose abdomen he pointed, and the man was attacked by dropsy, of which he died. When the third approached he pointed to the scar of a wound on the mocker's heel which had been inflicted years ago, and this wound opened again and killed him. When the fourth passed by he pointed to the sole of his foot, and afterwards a thorn penetrated it and the man died. When the fifth mocker passed by he pointed to his head and it began to ferment with poison and he died.

Khadija, the wife of the apostle, and Abu Talib, his uncle and protector, died in the same year, and after that calamities followed because in losing his wife the apostle of Allah lost his faithful supporter in Islam, and in losing his uncle he lost his defender against the people. This happened three years before the emigration to Medina. After the death of Abu Talib the Quraysh heaped insults upon the apostle of Allah which they would not have attempted during his life, and one of the fools among the Quraysh even went so far as to strew dust on his head. The apostle went with the dust on his head to his own house, and one of his daughters washed it off and wept; but the apostle of Allah said, 'Do not weep, my daughter. Allah will protect thy father.' And he added, 'The Quraysh would do nothing disagreeable to me until Abu Talib died.'

Once, when Muhammad had asked the nobles 'Will you say "There is no god but Allah?" and abandon whatever you worship besides Him?' Abu Talib had said, 'Nephew! In my opinion, you have asked them to do something extraordinary!' When Abu Talib uttered these words the apostle of Allah conceived hope for him and exclaimed, ' Then, uncle! Pronounce that phrase, and it will procure you redemption on the day of resurrection!' When he perceived Muhammad's anxiety to convert him Abu Talib said, 'O son of my brother, if I feared not such curses as will fall upon you and the sons of your father after I am dead, and that the Quraysh would suppose I had submitted from fear of death, I would pronounce it just to please you.'

When Abu Talib was on his deathbed, al-Abbas saw him move his lips and, having bent towards him, said to Muhammad, 'By Allah! My brother has uttered the phrase which you desired him to speak.' But the apostle of Allah replied, 'I did not hear it.' And Abu Talib died.

After the death of Abu Talib, when the apostle began to meet with such persecution from the Quraysh as he never had before, he went out to al-Taif [the nearest city of importance] in search of aid and protection from the Thaqif, in the hope that they would accept the revelation he brought from Allah. He went out to them quite alone.

He sat down with the three brothers who were the princes of
the Thaqif and invited them to Allah, and told them he had come
to ask their aid in the propagation of Islam, and their support
against those of his people who opposed him. But one of the men
said he would tear up the cloth which covered the Kaba if Allah
had sent him; and the second man said, 'Could Allah find no
better to send except you?' and the third man complained, 'I
shall never speak to you! For, if you are an apostle of Allah, your
dignity is too great for me to contradict you; and if you are lying,
there is no necessity for me to speak to you.'

So the apostle of Allah left them, in despair of receiving any
aid from the Thaqif. He said to them, 'Since you have done what
you have done, at least keep my request secret', for he was unwilling that his people should hear of the matter lest they be
further incensed against him. The three princes did not keep
silent, however, but encouraged their slaves to curse him and to
shout after him, so that he was compelled to take refuge in an
orchard belonging to Utba and Shayba, both of whom were
there at the time. The rabble of Thaqif withdrew and the apostle
of Allah sat down in the shade of a vine while Utba and Shayba
looked on.

When he felt himself safe the apostle cried, 'O Allah! To thee
I complain of my weakness, lack of resource, and helplessness
before men. O most merciful Allah! Thou art the Lord of the
weak! Thou art my Lord! If Thy wrath is not upon me, I care
not for persecution; I fly for refuge to the light of Thy countenance, which illuminates darkness and regulates this world
and the next. There is neither might nor power except with
Thee!'

Utba and Shayba were moved with compassion for the
apostle and told their Christian slave, Addas, to pluck a bunch
of grapes, place it in a dish, and take it to him. Addas placed the
dish before the apostle of Allah, telling him to eat, and the apostle
put his hand into the dish, said, 'In the name of Allah!' and began
to eat. Addas gazed at him and said, 'These are words uncommon
to the people of this country', and the apostle of Allah asked him
from which country he came and what was his religion; Addas

replied, 'I am a Christian from Nineveh.' The apostle of Allah said, 'From the town of the pious Jonah? He is my brother; he is a prophet and I am a prophet!' and Addas bowed down and kissed the head, the hands, and the feet of the apostle.

When Addas returned to the brothers they said, 'Woe betide you! Why did you kiss the head of that man, and his hands, and his feet?' He replied, 'O my masters! There is no finer man on earth than he! He has told me what none but a prophet can know', but they said, 'Let him not turn you away from your religion; for it is better than his.'

Then the apostle of Allah returned to Mecca, but his people were even more violent in their resistance and opposition, save only a few poor people who believed in him. He was in the habit of presenting himself at the time of seasonal fairs to the Arab tribes, in the following manner. He would stand before the Arab encampments and say, 'I am an apostle from Allah to you and command you to adore Allah and not to bestow this adoration on any other; to renounce the worship of idols; to believe me, His apostle, and to defend me that I may explain to you the revelation with which Allah has sent me.' But sometimes there stood behind him a shrewd-looking, well-dressed man, wearing a cloak, and with a lock of hair on each cheek, who addressed the people as soon as the apostle of Allah had ended his discourse. 'This man,' he would say, 'invites you to cast off al-Lat and al-Uzza, your allies among the djinns, in favour of his own invention and falsehood! Neither obey nor hear him!' This man was Abu Lahab, an uncle of the prophet.

For some time the apostle had little success with the tribes, although in the case of the Banu Amir one man among them said, 'By Allah! If I could take this man away from the Quraysh and have him on my side I could eat up all the Arabs with him!' He went on, 'If we pay homage to your religion, and Allah aids you to victory, what then?' and Muhammad replied, 'The dominion is Allah's! He placeth it where He willeth.' And the man exclaimed, 'If you expect us to make ourselves targets for the Arabs, but offer us no certainty of dominion in the case of victory, we have no need of your religion!' So they rejected him.

But when the Banu Amir returned home they went, as was their custom, to tell an aged sheikh what had taken place during the pilgrimage. When they went to him that year they told him, 'A fellow of the Quraysh came to us, saying that he is a prophet. He asked us to defend him, to join him, and to take him to our country.' The sheikh placed his hands upon his head, saying, 'Could it have been otherwise? Can the escaped bird be caught again? I swear that no Ismaili ever falsely claimed to be a prophet. He spoke truth. Where was your sense? It had deserted you.'

The apostle of Allah never failed to attempt the conversion of any man of note or position who came to Mecca.

When Abul-Haysar came to Mecca with members of his tribe, seeking an alliance with the Quraysh, the apostle of Allah heard about the visit, sat down with the men, and said, 'Are you willing to accept something better than that which you have come for?' They asked what that might be and he replied, 'I am an apostle of Allah, sent by Him to mankind in order to invite them to adore Allah and none other; and He has revealed a scripture to me.' Then he told them of Islam, and recited the Koran, and one young man said, 'By Allah! This is something better than what we came for!' But Abul-Haysar threw a clod of earth at the boy and bade him be silent. The young man died some months later, and people who were present told how he never ceased to speak of the name and virtues of Allah even at the very moment of his death. They had no doubt that he was a Muslim, because he had learnt the tenets of Islam during his single meeting with the apostle of Allah.

When Allah at last decided that the moment had arrived to glorify His prophet, and to fulfil His promise to him, the apostle of Allah went forth during the season of pilgrimage, as was his custom, to introduce himself to the Arab tribes, and met a small company of the Khazraj whom Allah had destined for favour.

When the apostle of Allah met them at al-Aqaba he asked, 'Are you allies of the Jews?' and they said, 'Yes.' They sat down with him and he invited them to believe in Allah, expounded Islam

to them, and recited the Koran. Now, Allah had ensured that
the Jews who lived in the country of the Khazraj, and who were
possessed of the scripture (whereas the Khazraj themselves were
polytheists and idolaters), should always say whenever a quarrel
broke out between them and the Khazraj, 'A prophet will soon
be sent and we shall become his followers and kill you with his
aid.' So when the apostle of Allah spoke to these men of the
Khazraj and invited them to believe in Allah they said to one
another, 'This is the prophet with whom the Jews have threatened us. We must forestall them and join him before they do.'
Accordingly they accepted Islam, saying, 'We have left our
people, for there is no tribe so divided by enmity and wickedness
as they. Perhaps Allah will unite them through you. We shall go
to them and urge them to accept your views and this religion,
so that, if Allah unites them around you, none will be more
exalted than yourself.' Then they returned to their country as
believers.

When they reached Medina they spoke of the apostle of Allah
and invited their people to accept Islam, so that acquaintance
with it spread until there was not one among the dwellings of all
their families in which the name of the apostle of Allah had not
been spoken. The converts in Medina became known as the
Helpers.

The next year [AD 621], when the season of pilgrimage came
again, twelve men of the Helpers met the apostle at the hill of
al-Aqaba; this is called the meeting of 'the first hill'. 'We paid
homage to the apostle of Allah after the unmilitant manner of
women – this happened before war was made incumbent upon
us. We pledged that we should not associate other gods with
Allah, nor steal, nor commit fornication, nor kill our female
children, nor tell lies, nor disobey what was right. If we fulfil
these conditions paradise is to be ours; if we transgress and suffer
punishment in this world, it will be an expiation; but if our sin
remains concealed till the day of resurrection, the affair rests with
Allah to punish or forgive.'

When the men left, the apostle of Allah sent Musab with them
to read the Koran to them, to teach them Islam, and to give them

instruction in religion; therefore Musab was known in Medina as 'The Reader'.

One day Musab went out with Asad, one of the Helpers of 'the first hill', and they entered an orchard and sat down near a well called Maraq, where several men who had made profession of Islam gathered around them. The princes of the Banu Abdul-Ashhal at that time were Sad b. Muadh, a cousin of Asad, and Usayd b. Hudayr, both of them idolaters like the rest of their people. They heard of the arrival of Asad and Musab, and Sad said to Usayd, 'Go to these two men who have come here to fool the weakminded among our people! Drive them away and forbid them to approach our dwellings. If Asad were not one of my kinsmen, I would have spared you this errand, but he is my cousin and I prefer to avoid him on this subject.' Accordingly Usayd took a sword and went to them; and when Asad saw him he said to Musab, 'This is the prince of his tribe. Show him the truth of Allah!' Musab replied, 'If he sits down I shall speak to him.' But Usayd remained standing in front of them, casting insults, saying, 'What has brought you here? Will you mislead the weakminded among our people? Leave us if you value your lives!' Musab replied, 'Sit down and listen; and if you are pleased with what you hear, accept it, but if you are displeased, that will put an end to the matter!' Saying, 'You have spoken well', and planting his sword in the ground, Usayd sat down, and Musab told him of Islam and recited the Koran. Then Usayd exclaimed, 'How beautiful and wonderful this is! What must one do to enter into this religion?' He was told, 'Wash yourself and purify your garments, then make profession of the truth, and pray.' Accordingly he rose, washed himself, purified his garments, made profession of the truth, and then prayed with two prayer-flexions.

After that, Usayd said, 'Behind me there is another man. If he were to follow you, not one of his tribe would fail to do the same. I shall send him to you now. His name is Sad.' Then he took his sword and departed to Sad and his tribe, who were sitting in their assembly; when Sad saw him, he exclaimed, 'Usayd returns with a different countenance from that he departed with.

What have you done, Usayd?' He replied, 'I conversed with the two men, and I have seen no evil in them. I told them they must not stay, and they said, "Do what you will." '

Sad jumped up angrily and snatched the sword from Usayd's hand, saying, 'By Allah! I think you have done nothing worth doing.' But when he approached the two men he realised that Usayd had merely enticed him there to hear what they had to say, so he stopped short and began to insult them. He said to Asad, 'If we were not kinsmen, you would not have dared to insult us in our own homes.' Musab replied as he had done to Usayd. At last, Sad asked, 'How does one make profession of Islam and enter into this religion?' Musab and Asad told him, and he rose, washed himself, purified his garments, made profession of the truth, prayed on his knees, took up his sword and returned with altered countenance to his people. He asked them, 'What is my position among you?' and they replied, 'You are our prince! The most loved, the most wise, and the most beneficent among us!' He continued, 'It will not now be right for me to speak to any of you until you believe in Allah, and in his prophet.' Thus, that evening, there was not a man nor a woman in the tribe who had not made profession of Islam.

Then Asad and Musab returned to their place and remained there, inviting the people to Islam till not a dwelling among all the tribes of the Helpers remained which did not include Muslim men and women, except only those few groups whose poet and leader was Sayfi. He was obeyed and followed by them and he kept them away from Islam until the apostle of Allah himself emigrated to Medina, and until the battles of Badr, Uhud, and the Ditch had been fought.

While Musab and the Medina converts – the Helpers (or Ansar) *– were having considerable success at Medina, the apostle in Mecca fared no better than before. It was a period of waiting and watching. Muhammad looked more and more eagerly to Medina and the north. The next vital part of the legend – the 'night journey and ascension to heaven' – further reflects the way in which his creed, even in the twelfth year of his mission, remained associated in his* *mind with Jewish and Christian doctrine: he still regarded the Jews and Christians as possible allies against the idolaters.*

The apostle of Allah said, 'While I was asleep within the northern enclosure of the Kaba, Gabriel came and kicked me with his foot. I sat up, but perceived nothing; therefore I again laid myself down. He came again and the same thing happened again, but when he kicked me the third time he took hold of my arm, so that I rose and went with him to the gate of the mosque. And lo! There I saw a beast, white in colour, resembling part mule and part donkey, with two wings covering its hind legs, and with its forelegs placed as far as its sight could reach. [This was Buraq, the animal on which all prophets before Muhammad had been conveyed.] When I approached the beast to mount, it became restive, but Gabriel placed his hand on its mane and said, "Art thou not ashamed, o Buraq? No servant of Allah has yet ridden thee who is more favoured than Muhammad!" Then the beast became steady, and I mounted it.'

The apostle of Allah, accompanied by Gabriel, was transported to Jerusalem, where he found Abraham and Moses and other prophets. He went to them and prayed with them; then two vessels were brought, one containing wine and the other milk. The apostle drank of the milk, but touched no wine, and Gabriel said, 'Thou art guided to the fundamentals of religion and thy people likewise; wine is prohibited to them.'

Then the apostle of Allah returned to Mecca, and in the morning he told the Quraysh what had happened to him; but most of them exclaimed, 'This is obviously nonsense! Caravans take a month to travel from Mecca to Jerusalem and another to return! Could Muhammad go there and return in a single night?' And many believers lapsed from the faith, and others went to Abu Bakr and said, 'What is your view concerning Muhammad, who imagines that he went last night to Jerusalem, where he prayed, and again returned to Mecca?' Abu Bakr replied, 'If he himself has said so, he spoke the truth! What is there to astonish you in this? By Allah, he tells me that revelation comes all the way from heaven to him on earth in a single hour of the night or the day, and I believe him! And this is a greater distance than the one which astonishes you.' Then he betook himself to the apostle of Allah and said, 'Describe Jerusalem to me; I have been there.' The apostle of Allah said, 'It was lifted up to me so that I might look at it', and he described the town in such a manner that Abu Bakr said, 'You have spoken the truth! I testify that you are an apostle of Allah!' And every part of the town Muhammad described, Abu Bakr confirmed, saying, 'You have spoken the truth! I testify that you are an apostle of Allah!' When he had finished his description the apostle said, 'And thou, o Abu Bakr, art also truthful', and on that day he surnamed him *Assidiq*, The Truthful One.

The apostle of Allah was in the habit of saying: 'My eye sleeps, while my heart is awake', but Allah knows best whether what was revealed to him took place in waking or sleeping state. The apostle of Allah gave his companions a description of Abraham, Moses and Jesus, as he saw them during that night. 'As to Abraham, I have never seen a man more resembling your companion [Muhammad] than he, nor your companion [Muhammad] resembling any other more than he. But as for Moses, he is a tall, dark, lively man with curled hair and a long nose; and Jesus, the son of Mary, is neither tall nor short, with flowing hair, and a countenance shining as if he had just come out of a bath, and you would imagine that water is dripping from his head although there is none on it.'

The apostle himself, according to his adopted son, Ali, 'was neither too tall nor too short, he was of a middling stature; his hair was neither too curly nor too flowing, it was like the hair of any other man. He was neither too plump nor too fat, and his complexion was pale, with a tinge of red. His eyes were large and black, his lashes long, his head and shoulder-bones large, and the hair of his breast was scanty. His hands and feet were strong, he walked as if wading in water, and when he looked at anything he turned his whole person towards the object. Between his shoulders was situated the seal of prophecy, he being the last of the prophets, the most open-handed of men, the most courageous, the most truthful in speech, the most faithful in protection, of the mildest disposition, and most gracious in converse. Whoever saw him unawares was awe-struck, but those who conversed with him loved him.' Ali concluded, 'I have neither before, nor afterwards, seen the like of him.'

But neither the description of Jerusalem nor of the prophets convinced the people, so Muhammad continued, 'I passed near a caravan of one tribe in a valley, and the sound of my beast startled them so that a camel ran away; and I found it and directed them to it. And when I was in Dajanan I met a caravan of another tribe, and found the people asleep. They had a covered water-vessel which I opened; I drank the contents, and covered it again as it had been. Their caravan is now arriving through the pass, led by a dark camel loaded with two bags, one of which is black and the other reddish-brown.' The crowd hastened up to the pass, where the first sight they saw was the camel he had described. Then they asked the caravan about the water-vessel, and were told that the tribe had put it down covered, and full of water, but although the cover was in the same state when they awoke, the water was gone. When the second caravan arrived in Mecca they confirmed Muhammad's other story, saying: 'He has spoken the truth. He did indeed scare us in the valley and a camel ran away, but we heard a man's voice calling us to it, and we found it.'

The apostle of Allah further said: 'When I had ended my visit to Jerusalem a ladder was brought to me, the like of which for beauty I had never seen before. This is the ladder which the dead yearn to see brought forth [that they may mount to heaven on the day of the last judgement]. Gabriel made me ascend this ladder until we arrived at that gate among the gates of heaven which is called The Gate of the Keepers. Over this, an angel of angels presides, whose name is Ismail and who commands 12,000 angels each of whom also commands 12,000. The hosts of Allah are known to Himself alone! When he took me in Ismail asked: "Who is this, o Gabriel? Has a prophetic mission been conferred upon him?" Gabriel said: "Yes", and then Ismail congratulated me.

'The angels met me when I entered those heavens which are

closest to earth, and not one addressed me without smiling and
congratulating me, until an angel of the angels met me who
spoke to me and invoked happiness for me as they had done, but
he neither laughed nor was pleased like the others. Therefore I
asked, "O Gabriel! Who is this angel who has spoken to me like
the others, but neither smiled nor manifested any signs of
pleasure as they did?" Gabriel replied, "If he had ever laughed
before, or was destined ever to laugh in the future, he would have
laughed with thee now; but he never laughs; he is Malik, the
keeper of fire." Then I asked Gabriel who is empowered by Allah
to be obeyed in that heaven I now describe to you and who is,
moreover, the faithful servant of Allah, "Wouldst thou order him
to show me the fire?" He said, "Show Muhammad the fires of
hell!" Accordingly Malik removed the cover thereof, and it
raged and ascended in such a manner that I thought it would
devour all that I saw. Therefore I cried, "Order him to confine
it again!" and the angel said, "Retire!" Then the fire returned
to the place it had issued from, and when he replaced the cover
upon it I cannot compare its disappearance with anything but
the falling of the shadow of night.

'When I entered the heaven which is next to the earth I
beheld a man sitting therein, to whom the souls of men are
delivered. With some of these he was pleased, and said, "A good
soul issued from a good body." To others, however, he said
with a frown on his countenance, "A wicked soul departed from
a wicked body." I asked, "Who is this?" and Gabriel replied,
"This is thy ancestor Adam, to whom the souls of his progeny
are delivered; and if a faithful soul arrives he is pleased, but when
an unbeliever's soul passes he is displeased and grieved."

'After that I beheld men with lips like the lips of camels,
having their hands filled with lumps of fire which they stuffed
into their own mouths. The lumps of fire issued again from the
other end of their bodies. I asked, "Who are these, o Gabriel?"
and he replied, "These have wrongfully devoured the property
of orphans!"

'Next I observed men with bellies the like of which I had
never seen, and on the road were crocodiles rushing upon them

like mad camels and driving them into the fire, trampling upon them so that they could never escape from it. I asked, "Who are these, o Gabriel?" and he replied, "They are usurers."

'After that, I beheld men who had before them nice plump meat and at their sides foul and putrid meat, but they ate of the latter and abstained from the former. I asked, "Who are these, o Gabriel?" and he replied, "They are those who abandon the women Allah has permitted to them, and go instead to those whom Allah has prohibited to them." Then I saw women hanging by their breasts and asked, "Who are these?" And Gabriel replied, "They are women who attribute to their husbands children they did not father." The wrath of Allah is very great towards a woman who introduces into the family one who does not belong to it, to eat up their plunder and to observe their nakedness.

'After this, Gabriel took me up to the second heaven, and it contained the two cousins, Jesus the son of Mary, and John the son of Zakariah. Then he lifted me to the third heaven where I saw a man with a countenance like the full moon, and asked, "Who is this, o Gabriel?" and he replied, "This is thy brother prophet, Joseph son of Jacob." Next he made me ascend to the fourth heaven, where one man appeared, and when I asked, Gabriel said, "This is Idris." Then he raised me to the fifth heaven, which contained an aged man with white hair and flowing beard. I have never seen an old man more beautiful than he, and when I asked Gabriel, he said, "This is the beloved of his nation, Aaron son of Imran." And he raised me to the sixth heaven, where there was a dark man with a long nose. I asked, "Who is this, o Gabriel?" and he replied, "This is thy brother Moses, son of Imran." Then he made me go up to the seventh heaven, where I beheld an old man seated on a chair near the roof of the heavenly Kaba, which is entered daily by 70,000 angels who will not leave it till the day of the resurrection. I have never seen a man resemble your companion [Muhammad] more closely, nor your companion resemble anyone more than he. I asked, "Who is this, o Gabriel?" and he said, "This is thy ancestor Abraham."

'Then Gabriel entered paradise with me, where I saw a black houri and asked her, "Who art thou?" because she took my fancy as soon as I perceived her. She said, "I am destined for Zayd b. Haritha." ' Zayd, the freedman of the apostle, rejoiced at these glad tidings.

According to tradition, Gabriel did not ascend to a single heaven of the heavens without being asked 'Who is this, o Gabriel?' When he replied, 'Muhammad', he was again asked, 'Has he really been sent as a prophet?' Then he was welcomed with, 'Allah greet him on the part of his friend and brother.' This lasted till they arrived in the seventh heaven, where the apostle met his Lord, who made fifty daily prayers incumbent upon him.

The apostle of Allah continued his story. 'Then I began my return. When I passed near Moses, who was a good friend to man, he asked, "How many prayers have been made incumbent upon thee?" and I replied, "Fifty prayers every day." Moses said, "Prayer is heavy, and thy people are weak. Go to thy Lord and ask Him to lighten it for thee, and for thy people." Accordingly I returned to my Lord and asked Him to alleviate it for me and for my people. And He deducted ten. I went away again and passed near Moses, who repeated what he had said before. So I returned and asked my Lord, who once more deducted ten; and I went back to Moses, who sent me many times to Allah with the same injunction, until so many prayers were deducted that only five prayers remained for each day and night. On this last occasion, when I returned to Moses, he repeated his words once more, but I said to him, "I have gone back to my Lord and asked him so many times that I am ashamed; therefore I shall do it no more." Nevertheless, whosoever among you recites these five prayers, believing wholly in their efficacy and validity, will receive the reward due for the fifty prayers originally prescribed.'

At the season of pilgrimage [AD 622] Musab returned to Mecca with many of the Helpers as well as some idolaters. One who was there recorded: 'We went on the pilgrimage and promised to meet the apostle of Allah at the hillside [al-Aqaba]. When the agreed night had set in we kept our errand secret from those of our people who were idolaters, except from Abdullah b. Amr, the prince. To him we said, "You are one of our princes and nobles! We fear that as an idolater, you will hereafter become fuel for the fire!" and we invited him to accept Islam and told him of our impending meeting with the apostle of Allah at the hillside. Then he made profession of Islam and came with us to the meeting. We lay down that night as if to sleep with our people and baggage, then left silently for the trysting-place. We travelled warily and secretly like the sandgrouse, until we reached the pass by the hillside; there were seventy-three men of us, and two of our women.

'The apostle of Allah came with his uncle al-Abbas, an unbeliever who nevertheless wished to see his nephew conclude a firm alliance. Al-Abbas spoke first, saying, "You know that Muhammad is our kinsman! We have protected him against those of our own people who oppose him. He enjoys dignity among his people, and protection in his country; nevertheless, he shuns them and wishes to ally himself with you. If, therefore, you think you can keep your promise and protect him against his enemies, you may assume the burden you have undertaken; but if there is any likelihood of your surrendering and abandoning him after he has gone over to you, then leave him be, for he is safer among his own people." Then we asked the apostle for his opinion and he said, "I call on you to protect me as you would protect your own women and children!" A man called al-Bara then took hold of his hand, and swore, "We shall protect you against everything from which we protect our own selves. Accept therefore our allegiance. We are warriors who have inherited the right to arms."

'This speech was interrupted by Abul-Haytham, who said, "We have ties with other men (he meant the Jews) which we should have to sever. If we do this, and Allah aids you to victory, will you not return to your own people and abandon us?" The apostle of Allah smiled and replied, "By no means. Blood is blood, and shedding is shedding; you belong to me and I to you.

I shall fight those whom you fight, and I shall be at peace with
him who is at peace with you. Bring me twelve leaders who may
be charged with their people's affairs." And they brought nine
men from the Khazraj tribe and three from the Aus tribe.

'The apostle of Allah said to the twelve leaders, "You are the
sureties for your people just as Jesus' disciples were, and I stand
surety for my people." And they agreed.

'Al-Abbas asked the people, "Are you aware of the conditions
on which you pledge allegiance to this man? You pledge yourselves to him, to wage war against all and sundry. If your possessions should be ruined by misfortune and your nobles slain, and
you should give him up, then you will reap shame in this world and
the next. If, however, you think you can keep your promises in
the face of all misfortune, then it will profit you in this world and
the next." They replied, "We shall take him even at the risk of
losing all else", and turning to the apostle they asked, "But
what will be our reward if we keep our promise?" He replied,
"Paradise!" and they said "Stretch forth thy hand", and paid
him homage.'

When Allah gave His apostle permission to wage war, the
promise to fight immediately became a condition of allegiance to
Islam. This had not been so at the first meeting on the hillside,
when homage was paid 'in the manner of women'; Allah had
not then given His apostle permission to fight. He had given
permission neither to wage war nor to shed blood, but only to
call men to Allah, to endure insults patiently, and to pardon the
ignorant. Some of the followers of the apostle had therefore been
forced to flee from persecution into the countryside, some to
Abyssinia, others to Medina and elsewhere. When the Quraysh
rejected the mercy of Allah and spurned His prophet, they
tormented or drove away men who proclaimed the One-ness of
Allah, believed in His prophet, and adhered to His religion.

Allah therefore permitted Muhammad to fight and to aid his
followers against those who tyrannized over them. The first
verse which came down permitting him to wage war and to shed
blood began, 'Permission is granted unto those who fight
because they have been oppressed, and Allah may aid those who

have been driven from their homes merely for saying "Our Lord is Allah".' The verse continued by explaining that they had committed no crime against the people except that they worshipped Allah, and when they made Islam universal they would observe the appointed times of prayer, give alms, and enjoin all men to do good and to abstain from evil. Then a further verse was recorded: 'Fight against them until there be no more temptation' – until Believers shall no more be tempted to abandon their religion – 'and until the religion be Allah's', that is, until Allah alone shall be worshipped and none else besides Him.

Since permission to fight had now been granted, the apostle of Allah accepted allegiance at the second meeting on the hill only from people who swore to fight for him and his Lord against all men. He promised paradise as a reward.

'After the act of allegiance was over, Satan roared from the top of the hill in such a loud voice as I had never heard. He cried to the people of Mina [the surrounding countryside]: "Beware of this despicable apostate and his followers! Verily they are assembled to attack you!" And the apostle of Allah replied, "This is the Contemptible One of the hill. Hearken to me, o enemy of Allah! I shall make an end of thee yet!" Then the apostle told the people to depart to their caravans again, but one of them said, "If thou wish it, tomorrow we shall attack these people of Mina with our swords." The apostle of Allah replied, "We have not been commanded to do that." Accordingly we returned to our caravans and slept there till the morning.

'When we rose in the morning some of the most distinguished Quraysh paid our encampments a visit and said they had heard we meant to take Muhammad from them and had pledged ourselves to attack them. Then several of the idolaters among our people rose, knowing nothing of the night's work, and swore that such was not the case, and that we knew nothing about it. Herein they spoke the truth, but only on their own account.'

After the Helpers had left for Medina, the Quraysh made inquiries about the rumour and found confirmation of it. Accordingly, they set off in pursuit and overtook two of the twelve 'leaders'. One of these escaped, but they captured the other, tied his hands to his neck with thongs from his camel, and took him to Mecca, where they beat him and dragged him about by his abundant hair. Later he told how 'some Quraysh men approached and among them was one of handsome appearance, neatly dressed. So I said to myself, if there be good in any of these people, it will be in this man; but when he approached me he raised his hand, and struck me a violent blow. Then I said to myself, "There is no good among them." But one man had pity on me and said, "Is there no alliance between thee and any man of the Quraysh?" I replied, "There are some whom I have protected or defended against those who wished to oppress them in my country", and he said, "Then shout out the names of these men and tell what has taken place." So he went in search of them and they came and delivered me from the hands of the Quraysh, and I departed.'

When, on the hill, the Helpers swore allegiance to the apostle, to adopt Islam, to aid him and those who followed him as well as any other Muslims who might seek shelter with them, he ordered his companions and others who were with him in Mecca to emigrate to Medina, that they might meet their Helper brothers. He said: 'Allah has marked out for you kinsmen and homes where you may find refuge.' Accordingly, the Meccan followers left the city in groups. These were afterwards known as the Emigrants, and were then over one hundred in number.

But the apostle of Allah remained in Mecca, waiting for his Lord's command to leave Mecca and to migrate to Medina.

THE HIJRA

THE apostle of Allah remained in Mecca after his companions emigrated, awaiting divine permission to depart. None of his followers remained – except such as were forcibly prevented by the Quraysh or who had apostasized – but Ali, son of Abu Talib, and Abu Bakr, may Allah reward them both. Abu Bakr often asked the apostle for permission to emigrate, but he always received the answer, 'Be not in such haste; perchance Allah may give thee a companion', and Abu Bakr hoped that the companion might be Muhammad himself.

When the Quraysh saw that the apostle of Allah had gathered a united group and had gained adherents in another country, and when they saw his companions emigrating to that country, they realized that he had found shelter and protection. Accordingly they began to fear that the apostle of Allah might join his followers, and they knew that he was now determined to fight if necessary. They therefore met to consult on what they should do.

Satan himself greeted them at the door of their meeting-place in the guise of an aged sheikh, dressed in a cloak. When they asked him who he was, he replied, 'A sheikh who has heard of your intended discussion and has come to listen to what you say; and perhaps my opinion and advice will not be lost upon you.' So he entered with them.

When they all began to discuss the problem of Muhammad, one of them said, 'Put him in irons, imprison him, and wait till he dies, as has happened to other poets before him.' Then the sheikh exclaimed, 'No, by Allah! If you incarcerate him as you propose, the news will leak out to his companions and they will undoubtedly attack you and liberate him. Then, through his agency, they will so increase in number as to conquer you. This is not the thing to do; you must devise another plan!' They consulted further, and another man said, 'We shall expel him from our midst, and exile him from our country. After he departs, we care not where he goes nor what happens to him as long as we can arrange our affairs and re-establish peace amongst us.' The sheikh said again, 'No, by Allah! Do you not realize that by his fine conversation, his sweetness of speech, and his power over the hearts of men, he could conquer any Arab encampment in which he might settle; then the people would follow him, march against you, and deprive you of your supremacy. After that, he could deal with you just as he liked. Therefore think of another plan.'

Abu Jahl at last exclaimed, 'By Allah! I have a plan which none of you has yet thought of', and they asked, 'What is it, o father of wisdom?' He said, 'I propose that from every tribe we should take one young, powerful, well-born man. To each of these, we should give a good sword with which to strike Muhammad. So we shall be delivered of him, his blood will be divided among all the tribes, and his followers will not have the strength to make war on so many.' The sheikh said, 'I see no other plan', and the people adopted the proposal and then dispersed.

But Gabriel came to the apostle of Allah and said to him, 'Do not spend this night in thy accustomed bed.'

When a part of the night had elapsed the conspirators assembled at Muhammad's door to watch him, intending to fall upon him while he was asleep. When the apostle of Allah saw them he said to Ali, 'Sleep on my bed and cover thyself with my green cloak, and they will do thee no harm.' It was the custom of the apostle to sleep in that cloak. Meanwhile Abu Jahl jeeringly told the waiting conspirators, 'Muhammad says that if you follow him you will become princes both of the Arabs and the non-Arabs, that you will be resurrected after death, and given gardens like the gardens of Jordan; but if you do not follow him, he will kill you and after death you will be resurrected and burn in the fires of hell.'

The apostle went out to them and said, 'Yes! That is the truth', and Allah blinded them so that they could not see him. Then Muhammad scattered dust on their heads, recited a verse from the Koran, and went about his business.

After a while, a man came along and asked the still waiting conspirators, 'What are you waiting for?' and they replied, 'Muhammad.' 'May Allah confound you!' the man exclaimed. 'Muhammad came out to you, and scattered dust on the head of every man among you, and then went his way. Can you not see what has happened to you?' Every man placed his hand on his head, and found that dust was on it, and then they began to search around. Finding Ali on the bed, wrapped in the cloak of the apostle, they said, 'Here is Muhammad still sleeping in his mantle!' – and so they did not move until morning. But it was Ali who rose from the bed, and they realized that the man who had spoken to them had told the truth.

Allah now permitted His prophet to emigrate. Abu Bakr, who was a man of property, had in the hope of this eventuality purchased two camels which he had kept stabled and fed in preparation for an emergency. The apostle never failed to visit Abu Bakr either in the morning or in the evening, but on the day when Allah gave him permission to emigrate he arrived unexpectedly at noon. The apostle said to Abu Bakr, 'Allah has given me permission to depart and to emigrate', and Abu Bakr asked, 'In company, o apostle of Allah?' He replied, 'In company'. Then Abu Bakr wept for joy and said, 'I have kept these two camels in readiness for this!' Then they hired an idolater as guide and left the camels with him until they were ready to depart from the district.

No one knew of the departure of the apostle except Ali, and Abu Bakr and his family. Ali was ordered to remain in Mecca until he had returned all the goods which people had entrusted to the keeping of the apostle; there was not a man in Mecca who had property about which he was anxious who did not deposit it with Muhammad because of his renowned truthfulness and honesty.

When the time for departure came the apostle and Abu Bakr left Mecca by way of a gap at the rear of Abu Bakr's house and went to a cave on Mount Thaur, beneath Mecca. Abu Bakr instructed his son Abdullah to listen during the day to what people in Mecca were saying about them, and to bring them the news in the evening. He also ordered Amir, his freedman to pasture the sheep during the day, and bring them to the cave in the evening; and he told his daughter, Asma, to bring food at nightfall.

The apostle of Allah remained in the cave with Abu Bakr for three days. When the Quraysh missed him they offered a reward of one hundred camels to anyone who would bring him back; Abdullah, the son of Abu Bakr, brought this news. Amir, the freedman, pastured his sheep among the other shepherds of Mecca, but brought the flock to the cave at nightfall and they milked the flock and slaughtered some. When Abdullah went in the morning to Mecca, Amir followed him with the flock so as to conceal his tracks.

When three days had elapsed and the people ceased to inquire about them, the hired guide arrived with their two camels, and a third belonging to himself, and Asma, the daughter of Abu Bakr, came with provisions. But she had forgotten to bring a cord, and they could not tie the provisions to the camels until she removed her girdle and used it for a rope; therefore Asma became known as 'She of the Girdle'.

Abu Bakr offered the better of the two camels to Muhammad, but the apostle replied, 'I shall not mount a camel which is not my own'. Abu Bakr said, 'Then she is thine, for thou art as my father and mother to me.' The apostle refused the gift and asked what Abu Bakr had paid for the camel, saying, 'I shall accept her for that.' So they agreed, and then they mounted and set off, with the freedman Amir sharing Abu Bakr's camel.

Meanwhile, in Mecca, several Quraysh men paid a visit to the house of Abu Bakr. Asma, 'She of the Girdle', went out to them and they asked ' "Where is thy father, o daughter of Abu Bakr?" I replied, "I do not know where my father is." Then Abu Jahl, who was a brutal, wicked fellow, lifted up his hand and struck my cheek so violently that my ear-ring fell out.

'We remained three nights without knowing in what direction the apostle of Allah had gone, until a djinn arrived from the lower part of Mecca, reciting verses in the Arab manner. From him we learned where the apostle of Allah had gone, and that his destination was Medina.

'Abu Bakr took away with him all his property, amounting to five or six thousand *dirhams*. My grandfather, who was blind, came to us and said, "I think Abu Bakr has deprived you of his property as well as his person", but I replied, "By no means, grandfather. He left us a great deal." Then I took some stones and placed them in a hole where my father used to keep his valuables, and covered the hole with a cloth; and I took hold of my grandfather's hand, saying "Lay your hand upon this, father." When he had done so, he said, "There is nought ill; if he has left you this, he has acted well; it will suffice you." But in truth, he had left us nothing, and I dissimulated to ease the old man's mind.'

One man at least, Suraqa by name, determined to earn the promised hundred camels for capturing Muhammad. Having heard a rumour of the apostle's route, he ordered his horse, then 'put on my armour and consulted the arrows which foretell the future. But the one I did not wish to see, that which said "He will escape", came out. When I mounted my horse to pursue him it stumbled and I fell to the ground. I said to myself, "What is this?" and again took out my arrows. They gave me the same reply as before. Nevertheless, I continued to ride in pursuit of him; again my horse stumbled and fell. Once more I consulted my arrows, and once more they gave me the same reply. Nevertheless I mounted again to pursue him. When the little group of fugitives at last came in sight, my horse stumbled and its forefeet sank in the ground so that I fell; and when the horse pulled its forefeet out of the ground they were followed by clouds of dust as if there were a sandstorm. Then I knew that Muhammad was protected from me and that he would conquer.'

The apostle reached Medina eight days after leaving the cave, on a Monday when the sun was near the meridian.

When news reached Medina that the apostle had left Mecca, Abdul-Rahman told how the followers of the apostle 'used to go out after morning prayers, expecting his arrival. We went out to a stony plain to look for him, and did not move until the sun drove us into the shade; but if we could find no other shade we had to enter our houses, because it was the hot season. The first man who caught sight of him on the day he at last arrived was a Jew, who knew that we awaited the apostle of Allah; and he shouted at the top of his voice, "See! your good fortune has arrived!" We went out to the apostle, who was sitting in the shade of a date-palm with Abu Bakr, a man of the same age as he. As most of us had not seen the apostle of Allah before, the people could not distinguish him from Abu Bakr until the sun fell on the apostle and Abu Bakr rose to shelter him with his cloak. Then we knew which he was.'

Then the apostle of Allah took up his abode at Quba, two miles outside Medina, with Kulthum, a friendly chief, and Abu Bakr dwelt with Khubayb; and they were assured that all Medina waited to welcome them.

The apostle of Allah remained at Quba on Monday, Tuesday, and Wednesday, and on Thursday he laid the foundation of a mosque; on Friday he left for Medina, and, during the short journey, he prayed at the foot of the valley called Ranuna. These were the first Friday prayers he held in Medina.

Many tribes and families welcomed him and invited him to honour their houses, but he replied, 'Allow my camel to go where she will, because she is guided by Allah.'

At last the camel stopped in a courtyard which was part burial ground, part date-grove, part camel enclosure, and knelt down; then it rose and went on a short distance. But it looked backwards and returned to the place where it had first intended to stop; there it knelt down, murmured and placed its chest on the ground. So the apostle of Allah alighted and took up his lodgings at the house of Abu Ayyub, near the courtyard. He inquired to whom the courtyard belonged and was told to two orphans, named Sahl and Suhayl; so he bought it to build a mosque thereon.

Abu Ayyub records that, 'When the apostle of Allah had taken up his abode in my house, he dwelt below and I above. Then I said to him, "O prophet of Allah, who art dear to me as my father and mother; I dislike and think it sinful that I should be above thee and thou below me." But he replied, "It is more pleasing to us and to those who visit us, that we should be in the lower part of the house." Accordingly the apostle of Allah remained beneath and I above.

'We used to prepare his supper and send it to him. When he returned what he could not eat, both I and Umm Ayyub touched the spot where his hand had been; then we ate what he had left hoping thus to gain a blessing. We sent him one evening a supper into which had gone onions or garlic, and the apostle of Allah returned it, and we found no trace of his hand on it; therefore I went to him in terror and asked him the reason. He replied, "I found in it the smell of this plant, and I am a man who has close contact with others. But you may eat it." Accordingly we ate it, but never offered him that plant again.'

The apostle of Allah remained in Medina until the following year when his mosque and his dwellings were built. He worked on them with his own hands to encourage his followers. Islam in Medina soon became so complete that only a handful of houses remained whose tenants had not made profession of Islam.

The first public sermon delivered by the apostle was as follows. 'Send good works ahead of you for the benefit of your souls! When one of you is snatched off by death your Lord will say

unto you – for there will be no interpreter or chamberlain
between you and Him – "Has not my apostle come and preached
to thee? I have given thee possessions, and bestowed benefits
upon thee! What hast thou sent ahead for thy soul's reward?"
Then you will look to the right and to the left, but will see nothing. And you will look forward and see nothing but hell!

'But he who can give even a little piece of date, and does so,
will help to shade his countenance from the fire of hell; and he
who has nothing to give, let him shield himself by means of the
Good Word. For good is rewarded from tenfold to seven
hundredfold! Peace be unto you, and the mercy and blessing of
Allah!'

When the apostle of Allah addressed the people for the
second time he said, 'Let us take refuge with Allah from the
wickedness of our own souls, and from the evil of our own deeds.
He whom Allah guides, none can lead astray; and whom He
leads astray, none can guide. There is no god but Allah and He
has no companion. Verily, the finest words are the scripture
of Allah; blessed is the man whose heart Allah has adorned with
it, whom He has caused to profess Islam after unbelief, and who
has preferred it to all the other beliefs of men; indeed, it is the
best and most eloquent of all. Love what Allah loves. Love
Allah with all your hearts, and be not weary of the word of
Allah or the mention thereof; but let not your hearts be hardened
against it, because it is the most exquisite and high of all Allah
has created.

'Therefore adore Allah, and associate nothing idolatrous with
Him! Fear Him with the fear that is His due. Carry out towards
Allah all that you say you will, and love one another in the spirit
of Allah, because He becomes wrathful when His covenant is
broken. The peace of Allah be with you, and His mercy!'

*By no means all the inhabitants of Medina and the surrounding
districts were converts to Islam. Some idolaters remained, who
rallied round Abdullah b. Ubayy, a man of great authority in
Medina before the advent of the apostle and who remained a
continuing thorn in the flesh of his success. It soon became apparent,*

too, that some of the Helpers were not altogether convinced of the political wisdom of supporting the apostle: these came to be regarded as paying lip-service to Islam, but hiding treachery in their hearts, and they were known and reviled as 'the Hypocrites'. Finally, there were three Jewish tribes settled just outside the city. Since much of the apostle's authority claimed to be derived from the Jewish scriptures, he attempted to win the Jews over to his cause, as allies if not as Believers.

In Medina the apostle of Allah drew up a document concerning the Emigrants and the Helpers, and the making of a treaty with the Jews which would ensure to both sides the maintenance of their religion and possessions, and laid down certain conditions of the alliance.

'In the name of Allah the merciful, the compassionate! This concerns the Believers fled from Mecca and those of Medina, as well as those who follow them; join with them, and fight with them, for they are a community excluding all other men. The Emigrants from Mecca shall pay blood-ransom among themselves and redeem their prisoners with the righteousness and justice suitable among Believers. The Helper tribes of Medina shall do the same. Believers shall not abandon him who is destitute among them, but shall aid him with gifts, drawn either from the ransom of prisoners or the blood-ransom paid for persons slain.

'Believers shall guard against him who rebels, or seeks to spread enmity or wickedness among them; let every man's hand be against him, even should he be the son of a Believer. No Believer shall kill another for the sake of an infidel nor aid an infidel against a Believer. Verily, the protection of Allah is indivisible and extends to the meanest Believer of all; and each must befriend other Believers above all men.

'Jews who follow us shall be given aid and equality; they shall not be oppressed, nor shall aid be given to others against them.

'The safety of Believers is indivisible; no one shall be saved at the expense of another, when battles are being fought in the name of Allah, save with equity and justice. In every religious campaign, Believers must aid one another in avenging blood spilled in the way of Allah.

'No idolater is permitted to take under his protection any property, nor any person, belonging to a Quraysh Unbeliever, or to aid a Quraysh against a Believer. He who kills a Believer will himself be killed – unless his victim's kinsmen accept blood-ransom – and it is the duty of all Believers to exact the penalty. He who aids or shelters a malefactor will earn the curse and wrath of Allah on the day of resurrection, nor will there be any escape therefrom. If you are at variance on any matter, refer it to Allah or to Muhammad.

'The Jews will share the cost with the Believers as long as they fight a common foe; the Jews are one community with the Believers (but they have their own religion as the Believers have theirs). As with the Jews, so with their adherents, except for him who commits a crime.

'None shall depart to war except by the permission of Muhammad, but none shall be hindered from avenging an injury. He who does ill only brings ill upon himself and upon his family, unless he be oppressed; then Allah will justify his deed. There shall be mutual aid between Believers and Jews, in face of any who war against those who subscribe to this document, and mutual consultations and advice. No man shall injure his ally, and aid shall be granted to the oppressed. The Jews, when fighting alongside the Believers, will bear their own expenses. Medina shall be sacred territory to those who agree to this covenant.

'If there should be any differences of opinion concerning this covenant and its meaning, they must be placed before Allah and Muhammad the apostle of Allah.

'Neither the Quraysh nor those who aid them are to be protected. Mutual aid will be given by Believers and Jews against any who may attack Medina. If the Jews are called on by the Believers to make peace, they must comply; and if the Believers are called on by the Jews to make peace, they must agree, except in the case of a holy war. Every man shall be allotted his reward by his own tribe.

'Allah requires that this document shall be ratified and put into effect; but it will not protect the unrighteous or the sinner. Allah protects the just and the pious, and Muhammad is the apostle of Allah.'

Soon after the arrival in Medina, the apostle of Allah established 'brotherhood in Allah' between his companions of the Emigrants and the Helpers, saying, 'Become brothers in Allah! Two by two!' Then he himself took the hand of Ali and said 'This is my brother!' Thus the apostle of Allah – prince of apostles, leader of the pious, ambassador of the Lord of both worlds, he who has no peer in dignity, nor any equal among the servants of Allah – became the brother of Ali. Then the uncle of Muhammad, Hamza – the lion of Allah, and of His apostle – became the brother of Zayd, the freedman of the apostle of Allah; and Jafar – the two-winged, who was to soar in paradise – became the brother of Muadh; and Abu Bakr became the brother of Kharija. So it was with many others.

While the mosque was being built one of the first Medinan converts, Asad, died of a throat complaint, and the apostle foretold that his enemies would say he was powerless, that 'If he were truly a prophet, his companion would not have died.'

The tribe, whose leader Asad had been, asked Muhammad to appoint a new chieftain, but he replied: 'I know your needs and I shall be your chieftain.' In fact, the apostle was unwilling to exalt any man of them above the others. For centuries after, it was a boast of this tribe that the apostle of Allah had been their chieftain.

When the apostle of Allah had settled himself in Medina, had assembled his fellow refugees around him, and arranged the affairs of the Helpers, Islam became properly established. Prayers were regularly held; the poor-tax and the fasts were prescribed; laws were formulated, and what could and what could not properly be done was defined.

When he first arrived in Medina the people had assembled around him at the appointed times for prayer, without waiting for any summons, but now the apostle considered whether he ought to call the people to prayer by the sound of a trumpet, as is customary among the Jews; however, he disliked the idea. Then he ordered a wooden gong to be made, and one was fashioned for his use; but while this was being done, a man named Abdullah had a vision. He went to the apostle of Allah and said, 'A wanderer came to me last night, a man who wore two green garments and carried a gong in his hand. I said, "Wilt thou sell this gong?" and he asked me my purpose with it. I said, "We shall call to prayers with it", but he replied, "Shall I tell thee something better than that? Cry: Allah Akbar [Allah is greatest]! Allah Akbar! Allah Akbar! Allah Akbar! I testify that there is no god but Allah! I testify that Muhammad is the apostle of Allah! Come to prayer, come to prayer! Come to blessedness, come to blessedness! Allah Akbar! Allah Akbar! There is no god but Allah!" '

When he heard this Muhammad said, 'This is a true vision, if it pleaseth Allah. Arise therefore with Bilal, give him the words and let him shout them, because he has a better voice than thine.' When Bilal acted as muezzin [the caller to prayer] and shouted these words, Umar heard him and went to the apostle of Allah, trailing his cloak after him, and said, 'I swear by Him who sent thee, that I have had the same vision as Abdullah.' The apostle said, 'Praise be to Allah!'

A woman whose house was the largest near the mosque later told how thereafter Bilal daily proclaimed the morning prayers. 'He used to come in the morning, and sit in my house waiting for the morning star. On beholding it, he would stretch himself and say, "O Allah! I praise Thee and invoke Thy aid that the Quraysh may accept Thy religion." Then he would begin his call to prayer.'

Among the converts and inquirers who came to Medina seeking the truth of Islam were many whose stories were strange. One such was Salman the Persian.

Salman the Persian was the son of a rich man who loved him so intensely that he imprisoned him in the house. But one day Salman went out to visit his father's property and passed near a

Christian church where the people were at their prayers; he could not understand what they were doing, because his father had kept him incarcerated, and he entered the church to see. When he saw them, their devotions so pleased and impressed him that he remained till sunset. After this, his father placed fetters on his legs, and again imprisoned him, but he threw away the fetters and went to Syria, where he had been told the root of Christianity was.

There he served in succession five good and wise upholders of the faith. When the fifth felt death was near, Salman asked: 'To whom do you recommend me to go; what should I do now?' The wise one replied: 'My son, I know not whether anyone exists today who is of the same religion as we, and to whom I might order thee to go; but the time of a prophet of the religion of Abraham is near at hand. This prophet will arise in the Arab country, and will flee to a region situated within two stony ranges which contain date-trees. He is endowed with marks which cannot be concealed, consumes gifts but not alms, and bears the seal of prophecy between his shoulders. If thou art able to go to that country, do so.' He then died and was buried.

Then Salman said to some passing merchants: 'Take me to the country of Arabia, and I will give you all my cows and sheep.' But they took his goods and sold him as a slave. After a time he was resold and taken to Medina, and when he reached there he recognized it from the description of his dead master as the place where the prophet would appear.

Soon the apostle fled from Mecca to Medina, and Salman heard of 'a man who has this day arrived from Mecca, and is believed to be a prophet'. Salman gathered some dates, and when the evening set in, took them to the apostle of Allah, and said: 'It has reached me that you are a pious man, and have companions with you who are strangers and needy. These dates I intended for alms, but I consider you to be worthier of them than others.' Then he offered them to him, whereon the apostle of Allah said to his companions: 'Eat!' But he himself restrained his hand and abstained from eating. Then Salman said to himself: 'This is one sign.'

He went away and again collected some dates and when the apostle of Allah appeared again in Medina he paid him a visit, brought the dates, and said: 'I have seen that you do not eat what is given as alms; but this is a gift wherewith I intend to honour you.' Now the apostle of Allah ate, beckoned to his companions, and they ate with him; and Salman said to himself: 'This is the second sign.'

On another occasion he went to the apostle of Allah and walked in a circle around him to ascertain whether he could see on his back the seal mentioned to him by his master. When the apostle of Allah noticed this he knew that Salman desired to verify something which had been described to him. Accordingly he threw off his cloak and Salman beheld the seal and recognized it. Then Salman bent over to kiss it, and to weep. The apostle of Allah said, 'Turn round!' Salman obeyed, sat down in front of him, and told him his story, and the apostle of Allah was pleased that the companions had heard it.

But Salman remained a slave for another two years, until the apostle of Allah said, 'Purchase thy liberty, o Salman!' Salman accordingly made a bargain with his owner for three hundred date-trees to be planted in furrows, and forty ounces of gold. The apostle said to his companions: 'Aid your brother!' And some gave thirty, some twenty, some fifteen, and some ten trees to aid Salman; every man according to his ability, so that Salman collected three hundred plants. Then the apostle said: 'Go, Salman, and dig the furrows, so that I may plant with my own hands.' Accordingly Salman dug and his friends helped him. When Salman had terminated the work he went and informed the apostle of Allah. Then the apostle of Allah went forth with him; they brought him the plants, and he planted them with his own hands, until the work was completed, and not a single plant died, so that Salman had paid all the date saplings and only the money remained. But a nugget of gold as large as a hen's egg having been brought to the apostle of Allah he asked, 'What has the Persian done who was redeeming himself?' Accordingly Salman was sent for, and the apostle said: 'Take this and pay it for what thou owest, Salman!' Salman asked: 'What will this amount to in my debt?' and he replied: 'Take it, because Allah will aid thee with it to pay thy debt.' Therefore Salman took the lump and weighed it, and it weighed forty ounces. With this Salman paid his debt, and became free.

In spite of his covenant with the Jewish tribes, relations became progressively more strained. From the Jewish point of view, Muhammad daily moved farther away from Judaism as he became ever more positive in what he required of his followers: while, to the apostle, the Jews appeared overcritical of his claims, and the possibility of an alliance between the Jews and the Hypocrites was a continuing source of disquiet. In Ibn Ishaq's biography of the apostle the rift in a never very firm alliance is illustrated with innumerable anecdotes.

Some Jewish rabbis came one day to the apostle of Allah and said, 'Answer us four questions satisfactorily, and we shall believe in you.' The apostle replied, 'On the covenant of Allah? Then ask what you will.' They asked, 'Tell us how an infant can resemble its mother, when the seed comes from the man?' The apostle of Allah said, 'Do you not know that the seed of a man is white and thick, whereas that of a woman is yellow and thin, and that which prevails over the other imparts the resemblance? They exclaimed, 'That is the truth', and continued: 'Then tell us about thy sleep.' He said, 'My eyes sleep, but my heart is awake.' Then they asked: 'Tell us what Israel denied himself', and he replied, 'Do you not know that the food and drink he most relished was the flesh and milk of the camel; and when he fell prey to a disease and Allah delivered him, in gratitude he forswore the food and drink he liked most, the flesh and milk of camels.' They said, 'That is the truth.' Then they asked, 'Tell us about the Spirit?' He replied, 'It is Gabriel, who comes to me.' Then the rabbis said: 'Agreed. But Gabriel is an enemy to us, and comes with violence and bloodshed. If this were not so, we would follow thee!'

On another occasion the apostle of Allah wrote to the Jews of Khaybar in this manner. 'In the name of Allah the merciful, the compassionate! This is from Muhammad, apostle of Allah, friend and brother of Moses, who confirms the revelation which Moses brought! Verily, Allah says to you, men of the scripture – and you will find it in your scripture – "Muhammad is the apostle of Allah! Those with him are violent against Unbelievers but merciful to one another. You can see them kneeling or prostrated, suing for the bounty and approbation of Allah; their foreheads are marked by traces of that prostration. Allah promises to those who believe and do good works, forgiveness and a great reward." By Allah, and by that revelation which He has hitherto sent down to you, by Him who fed with manna and quails the tribes that went before you, and by Him who dried up the sea for your ancestors that he might deliver them from Pharaoh – I adjure you to tell me if you find in that revelation which Allah sent down to you, that you should believe in Muhammad. If you cannot find that in your scripture, no displeasure will fall on you. Guidance will be distinguishable from error, and I invite you to Allah and to His prophet.'

When the Christians of Najran came to the apostle of Allah, Jewish rabbis came also and they disputed before the apostle. One Jew said to the Christians, 'You are nothing!' and denied Jesus and the gospel; then a Christian said to the Jews, '*You* are nothing!' and denied that Moses was a prophet, and denied the Torah. Then Allah revealed the following verse. 'The Jews say the Christians are nothing, and the Christians say the Jews are nothing, yet they both base their arguments on scripture. They are ignorant, and Allah will judge between them on the day of the resurrection.'

Then the Jewish rabbis disputed with the Christians of Najran, saying, 'Abraham was no other than a Jew.' And the Christians from Najran said, 'Abraham was no other than a Christian.' Then Allah revealed the verse, 'Why do you quarrel about Abraham, when the Torah and the gospel were not sent down until after his time. You have disputed about things you know, why then do you dispute about things you know not? Allah knoweth, but you know not. Abraham was neither a Jew nor a Christian. He was an orthodox Muslim, and he was no idolater. Those closest to Abraham are those who follow him and this prophet, and those who believe. Allah is the protector of the faithful.'

Then a Christian asked Muhammad, 'Do you want us to worship you as we worship Jesus, son of Mary?' The apostle replied, 'Allah forbid that I should worship anyone besides Him, or command any other besides Him to be worshipped. Allah has not sent me to do that.'"

Seventeen months after the apostle arrived in Medina the *qibla* [the direction in which Muhammad and his followers faced during prayers] was changed from Jerusalem to Mecca. Several Jews came to him and taunted him: 'O Muhammad! What has turned you away from the *qibla* you used to face? You allege that you follow the religion of Abraham; return, then, to the *qibla* of the religion of Abraham, to which you turned before, and we shall follow you and believe in you.' But they slyly intended thus to turn him away from his religion. Then Allah revealed the words: 'Foolish men say "What hath turned them away from the *qibla* to which they prayed?" Reply, "Allah's is the east and the west, He leads whom He will to the straight path." ' And Allah said, 'Turn thy face to the holy mosque [the Kaba at Mecca]; and wherever you are, turn thy face to that.'

Once, Muadh asked some Jewish rabbis about a subject mentioned in the Torah, but they refused to answer him about it. So Allah revealed the verse, 'Those who conceal what We have sent down, after We have made it plain, will be cursed by Allah.'

Again the apostle of Allah invited the Jews, possessors of the scripture, to accept Islam and tried to enlist them in its favour; but he also threatened them with the punishment and vengeance of Allah. He was told, 'Nay. We shall follow that religion which our fathers professed, because they were more learned and better men than we are.' Allah the most high and glorious therefore sent down the verse which says, 'And when it is said to them "Follow that revelation which Allah has sent down", they say, "Nay, we shall follow that which we found our fathers practise." What? Though their fathers knew nothing, and were not rightly guided!'

On another occasion the apostle entered a Jewish school and

invited those who were present to Allah. They asked, 'What is your religion, Muhammad?' and he replied, 'The religion of Abraham.' They said, 'Abraham was a Jew.' Then the apostle of Allah told them, 'Bring the Torah and let that judge between me and you', but they refused.

Among the tribes who had professed Islam were the Khazraj and the Aus, who had formerly been in a constant state of enmity. One day a sheikh who hated Islam passed by and, seeing the new friendship between the tribes, became angry and decided to cause mischief. Accordingly, he beckoned to a young Jew and said, 'Go and sit with them; then mention the battle of Bu'ath and what preceded it!' Bu'ath was the day on which the two tribes, the Aus and the Khazraj, had fought; the Aus had been victorious. The young Jew did what he was told and the people began to talk on the subject, to dispute, and boast to one another, till at last two men jumped up, arguing hotly, and one said, 'If you wish, we shall repeat the battle!' Now, both parties became enraged and cried, 'The challenge is accepted! Outside the town! To arms! To arms!' and they all rushed off. As soon as the apostle of Allah heard of this, he went after them, and when he reached them he said, 'Do you now revive the disputes which raged during the years of idolatry? After Allah has led you to Islam and united you in friendship?' Then the people realized that this was a trick of Satan, and wept, and the Aus embraced the Khazraj and all departed with the apostle of Allah, attentive and obedient.

Some Muslims tried to keep up connexions with the Jews because of the alliance which had existed between them during the years of ignorance; but Allah revealed the following verse, prohibiting this kind of association. 'Contract no friendships except among your own number. Others would certainly corrupt you. They desire your humiliation; their hatred is clear enough in what they say, but what their hearts conceal is even worse. You have more right to hate them than they you. When they meet you they say, "We believe", but when they are alone they bite their fingers with rage against you. Say, "Die in your rage!" '

One day Abu Bakr entered the schoolhouse of the Jews and found many of them assembled around a man whose name was Finhas. He was a doctor and rabbi, and had with him another rabbi called Ashya. Abu Bakr said to Finhas, 'Woe betide thee. Fear Allah, and make profession of Islam!' Finhas replied, 'We have no need of Allah, but He has need of us! We do not beseech Him as He beseeches us. We are independent of Him, but He is not independent of us. If He were independent of us, He would not ask for our money as your master Muhammad does [for a war against Mecca]. He forbids usury to you, but pays us interest; if He were independent of us He would give us no interest.' At this, Abu Bakr became angry, and struck Finhas violently, saying, 'I swear by Him in whose hands my life rests that if there were no treaty between us I would have struck off your head, you enemy of Allah!' Then Finhas went to the apostle of Allah and said, 'See what your companion has done to me!' Abu Bakr explained what happened, but Finhas denied the whole matter and said, 'I spoke no such words!' But Allah revealed a verse confirming the words of Abu Bakr.

Early in Muhammad's stay at Medina the rabbis had met to judge a married man who had committed adultery with a Jewish woman who was also married. They said, 'Send this man and this woman to Muhammad, ask him for a judgement of the case, and let him prescribe the penalty. If he decides to condemn them to the *tajbih* – when criminals are scourged with a rope of date-fibres dipped in resin, then have their faces blackened and are placed on two donkeys with their faces turned towards the rump – 'then obey him, for he is a prince, and believe in him. But if he condemns them to be stoned, he is a prophet; then be on your guard against him, lest he deprive you of what you have.'

They had asked the apostle's judgement and he went to where the priests sat, and said to them, 'Bring me your learned men!' They brought him Abdullah b. Suriya, who was the most learned, though one of the youngest, among them. The apostle talked alone with him and had him confirm on oath that 'according to the Torah, Allah condemns to stoning the man who commits adultery after marriage'. Suriya added, 'They know you are an inspired prophet, but they envy you!' Then the apostle went out and ordered the culprits to be stoned in front of the door of his mosque. When the man felt the first stone he bent over his mistress to protect her from the stones, until they were both killed. This is what Allah did for His apostle, to exact the penalty for adultery from these two persons.

The apostle asked the Jews what had induced them to abandon the penalty of stoning for adultery, when it was prescribed in the Torah. They said the penalty had been observed until a man of royal blood committed adultery, and 'the king would not allow him to be stoned. When, after this, another man committed adultery and the king desired that he be stoned, they said, "Not unless you also permit the first man to be stoned." Then all agreed to resort to scourging, and both the memory and practice of stoning died out.' Then the apostle of Allah said, 'I was the first to revive the command of Allah, His scripture, and obedience to it.'

On another occasion a company of Jews came to the apostle and asked, 'Allah has created creation, but who created Allah?' And the apostle became so angry that his colour changed, and he leapt up in zeal for his Lord. But Gabriel came and quieted him, and said, 'Calm thyself, Muhammad!' Gabriel brought a reply from Allah to what they had asked him. 'Say "He is the one god! Allah is self-generating! He begetteth not, nor is begotten! And there is none equal." '

After he had recited this to them, they said: 'Describe Him to us, o Muhammad! What is His shape? His arm – what is the strength of His arm?' The apostle became even more wrathful and he leapt up once more; but Gabriel again came and told him to be calm and brought a reply from Allah. 'They have not properly understood the power of Allah! He will grasp the whole earth on the day of the resurrection, and the heavens will be rolled up in His right hand! Praised be He, and exalted above all their idols.'

A deputation of Christians from Najran, consisting of sixty

riders, arrived on a visit to the apostle; among them were four-teen of their most respected men, three of whom were entrusted with the management of their affairs. The leader of the people, the chief councillor whose advice they always followed, was Abdul-Masih. Their administrator was al-Ayham. Their bishop, scholar, religious leader and master of their schools, was Abu Haritha, who was respected among them and a renowned student with an extensive knowledge of their religion; the Christian princes of Byzantium had honoured him with gifts of goods and servants, built churches for him, and venerated him for his learning and religious zeal. On the way to visit the apostle, Abu Haritha said to his brother, 'This is the prophet whom we were expecting.' His brother rejoined, 'Then what hinders you from acknowledging him?' Abu Haritha replied, 'Those who have paid us respect, given us titles and shown us favours, are opposed to him; if I acknowledge him, they will deprive us of all we enjoy.'

When the delegation arrived in Medina they entered the mosque while the apostle was holding his afternoon prayers. When the time arrived for their own prayers they stood up in the mosque of the apostle and made their devotions; and the apostle of Allah said, 'It is permitted.' And they prayed with their faces towards the east.

The three leaders, although Christians, differed among them-selves on some points. They said that He was God [or 'Allah'], because He brought the dead to life, healed the sick, made known the unknown, created a bird from clay, breathed on it and gave it life; they said that He was also the Son of God because He had no known father and spoke in His cradle, which no human had ever done before; and they said, too, that He was the third of the Trinity, because the word of God was always '*We* have acted, *We* have commanded . . .' and if God were but one, His word would be '*I* have commanded, *I* have created . . .' Thus He is He, and He is Jesus and He is Mary.*

*Muhammad and his followers (and consequently his biographers) found the doctrine of the Trinity far from clear and often referred to Mary, mother of Jesus, as the third of the Trinity.

The apostle said to them, 'Resign yourself to the will of Allah' [he presumably meant 'Profess Islam', but the three leaders took the injunction at its face value], and they replied, 'We did so before thee.' 'You lie!' said Muhammad. 'You say that Allah has a son, you worship the cross, and you eat the flesh of pigs; these prohibit you from submission.'

Then Allah revealed the Sura known as *The Family of Imran* which begins by refuting the Christian Trinity, and proclaiming the omnipotence and one-ness of Allah. There is no god but He, the Living, the Eternal who cannot die; but Jesus died and was crucified. Allah has sent down the Koran, the criterion of truth and falsehood in matters of difference over Jesus and others. Those who disbelieve the directions of Allah will suffer grievous punishment; for Allah is mighty and avenging. Nothing is hidden from Allah on earth or in heaven and He knows what the Christians intend with their claims that Jesus is Lord and God. But Allah formed Jesus in the womb – this the Christians do not deny – as He formed other human beings; how, then, can Jesus be god?

It is Allah who has sent down the scripture with clear and categorical verses at the core. But other verses are obscure and convoluted and can be explained in several ways; and these are sent by Allah to test men. Those in whose hearts there is perversity will expound their own interpretation of them as if it were categorical truth, or clothe their own inventions in the obscurity of the verses. But truthful men balance the clear verses with the obscure and thus the parts of the scripture clarify each other; the argument is plain, the justification becomes evident, falsehood is removed, and unbelief is defeated.

Although Allah gave Jesus powers of various kinds (on the basis of which the Christians believe him to be God), it was in order to make him a sign to mankind, to furnish them with proofs of his prophetic mission. But Allah held back many manifestations of His dominion and power, such as the succession of day by night and night by day, and bringing forth the living from the dead and the dead from the living. Over none of these matters did He give power to Jesus, but all of these would have been at his disposal had he been God; instead, he fled from kings, from country to country.

Then Allah explained to them the origins of Jesus. Allah selected Adam and Noah, and the family of Abraham and the family of Imran above all other men, in successive generations. The wife of Imran dedicated the child in her womb to Allah, and when she was delivered of it she said, 'O Lord, I have brought forth a daughter. I have called her Mary, and I commend her and her issue to Thy protection.' Allah accepted her graciously, and made her grow to a goodly woman. Then the angels said to her: 'Allah has chosen thee and has purified thee. He has chosen thee above all other women. Bend down to the Lord and worship!' She said: 'Lord! How can I have a child when no man has touched me.' He said: 'Allah createth what He pleaseth.' Then He said: 'We shall teach him the scripture, and wisdom, and the Torah' – which had been with them from the time of Moses – 'and the gospel. And he will be an apostle to the children of Israel, saying, "I have come to you with a sign from your Lord. Allah is my Lord and your Lord, and I shall heal those who are blind from birth, and lepers. And I shall revive the dead with the permission of Allah, and will tell you of what you eat, and of what you store up in your houses. Herein will be a sign for you that I am an apostle from Allah, if ye are believers in the Torah."'

Allah took Jesus to Himself when they had determined to kill him. 'They devised a stratagem, and Allah devised a stratagem; but Allah is the best deviser of stratagems.' Allah lifted him up and purified him; 'the likeness of Jesus with Allah is as the likeness of Adam, whom He created of dust, saying "Be". And he was. I created Adam of dust, without the intervention of man or woman, and he became – like Jesus – flesh, blood, hair, and skin. So the creation of Jesus without a man is no more wonderful than that of Adam.'

After hearing this, the Christians said to Muhammad, 'Allow us to consider the matter and let us then return to tell you what we mean to do.' Then they discussed in private and Abdul-Masih said: 'You know that Muhammad is an inspired prophet;

and no nation ever cursed a prophet without its chiefs dying, and the number of its children diminishing. If you do this, you will perish; but if you do not curse him and yet wish to stay in your own religion, then take leave of the man and return to your own country.' Accordingly, they went to the apostle and said to him, 'We have decided to leave you in your religion, and to remain in our own; but send one of your companions with us and let him judge among us concerning all differences of property that may arise; for we are impressed with you.' The apostle of Allah agreed to their request.

Aisha, the daughter of Abu Bakr and now Muhammad's youthful wife, later told how 'When the apostle arrived in Medina, whose climate was unlike Mecca, fever was more prevalent than in any other place on earth, and the companions suffered and fell sick with it. Allah, however, guarded His prophet.' Abu Bakr and his two freedmen caught the fever, and Aisha 'went there and paid them a visit; at that time veils had not yet been commanded to us. They were stricken with violent fever, and when I asked my father "How art thou?" he replied, "A man may rise with his family in the morning, but death may be nearer to him than his sandal-strings." I decided my father knew not what he said, and went to his two freedmen; but they, too, spoke in riddles. So I told the apostle of Allah what I had heard them say, and he explained that they were delirious because of their high temperature and fever. The apostle prayed to Allah: "Make Medina as dear to us as Thou hast made Mecca, or more dear. Bless everything therein, and carry this epidemic away to another place." '

While this fever raged the apostle's followers were so weak that they had to pray sitting down. He visited them while they were praying thus and told them, 'The prayer of a seated man has only half the value of a prayer performed standing!' So the Muslims forced themselves, in spite of their weak and shaky condition, to pray standing, that they might gain merit.

A year after his arrival in Medina, and thirteen years after his 'call', the apostle of Allah prepared himself for war in obedience

to the command of Allah that he should attack the idolaters. He
was then fifty-three years old.

*Religious hostility and a measure of personal resentment against the
Quraysh idolaters were deeply implanted in the mind of the apostle.
He had sworn vengeance against them and, now that his followers
were settled in Medina, he felt the time had come to make good his
threats.*

*Not far from Medina was the main caravan route which the
Quraysh used in their trade with the north. Frankincense, silk,
precious metals and leather passed regularly back and forth between
Mecca, Syria, Abyssinia, and the Yemen. The prizes were too rich
not to add an irresistible weight to basically religious and political
impulses. And attack on the caravans of the Quraysh meant an
attack on what was simultaneously their weakest and most valued
link.*

This was the first occasion on which the white banner of
Muhammad was seen. Muhammad sent out from Medina sixty
or eighty of the Emigrants, led by Ubayda; none of the Helpers
accompanied them. They rode as far as the water in the Hijaz
and there found a great trading caravan of Quraysh from Mecca.
There was no battle, but Sad shot an arrow which was the first
arrow shot in Islam. Then the parties separated. Two men fled
from the Unbelievers to join the Muslims; these were al-Miqdad
and Utba.

At the same time, the apostle sent his uncle, Hamza, with
thirty riders to the sea-coast at al-Is; there they met a party of
three hundred men from Mecca, led by Abu Jahl, but a man
named Majdi – who was on good terms with both sides – mediated
between them and they separated without coming to blows.
Hamza also bore a white banner which had been tied on by
Muhammad, and some say that this was the first time the banner
was seen; but his expedition and that of Ubayda occurred at the
same time and this has caused the confusion.

The apostle himself next went forth in search of the Quraysh
and reached Buwat, in the direction of Radwa. But he returned
to Medina without encountering his enemies and remained in

Medina for some weeks before he again went forth. He passed through the valley of the Banu Dinar, then through Fayfau-l-Khabar, then halted under a tree in the valley of Ibn Azhar. Food had been prepared for him nearby; there he prayed, and there his mosque is. He and his companions ate, and the very spot on which his cooking-vessel stood is still known. He continued his journey until he reached al-Ushayra in the valley of Yanbu and remained there for a month, forming alliances with neighbouring tribes along the sea-coast, before returning to Medina. He encountered no enemies, the caravan from Mecca – commanded by Abu Sufyan – having passed before he reached al-Ushayra.

When he returned from the expedition to al-Ushayra, the apostle remained at Medina for only ten nights before he had to sally out against one Kurz, who had plundered the herds of Medina. He marched as far as the valley of Safawan in the region of Badr, but was unable to overtake Kurz, and returned to Medina, where he remained for a further two months. This was the first expedition to Badr.

Shortly after this expedition to Badr the apostle sent Abdullah b. Jahsh and eight Emigrants on a journey. He gave a letter to Abdullah, but ordered him not to read it till the end of a two days' march; he also told him to avoid giving offence to any of his companions.

After Abdullah had marched two days' journey, he opened the letter, and found it contained the following instructions: 'Go on to Nakhla, between Mecca and Al-Taif, and keep watch over the Quraysh there and bring back news of their business.' Abdullah said, 'I read and obey!' Then he told his companions about the letter, and added, 'He has also prohibited me from forcing any one of you to do anything against his will. If, therefore, any of you wishes to earn martyrdom, let him come with me; but if not, let him go back.' All his companions went with him, and none remained behind, but at Bahran two of the travellers lost the camel which they had been riding in turns and they fell behind to look for it. Abdullah marched on with the rest of his companions to Nakhla, where they came upon a Quraysh caravan laden with raisins, tanned hides, and various other goods, and accompanied by four men.

When the caravan saw Abdullah and his companions they were afraid because they had alighted so near to them, but when Ukkasha – whose head was shaved like that of a pilgrim – approached them, they recovered their confidence and said, 'These are pilgrims, and we need have no fear of them.'

This took place on the last day of the sacred month Rajab [October]. Abdullah and his companions conferred among themselves: 'If we allow these people to continue and reach sacred territory tonight, they will be safe from us; but if we attack them now, we profane the sacred month.' And they vacillated and hesitated to attack, but at last mustered up their courage and agreed to slay as many of the Quraysh as they could, and take possession of what they had with them. So Waqid shot an arrow and killed one of the Quraysh, two others were made prisoner, and the fourth fled.

Then Abdullah, with his companions, the caravan, and the prisoners, returned to Medina, saying, 'One fifth part of our plunder belongs to the apostle of Allah.' This was before Allah had made it incumbent on Believers to give up a fifth part of any booty to Him. One fifth of the caravan was set aside for the apostle of Allah, and Abdullah distributed the rest among his companions.

When they arrived in Medina, however, the apostle said, 'I did not command you to fight in the holy month', and he walked away from the caravan and the prisoners, and refused to take anything from them. The captors were crestfallen and decided they were doomed, and their Muslim brethren, too, reproved them for their deed. In Mecca, the Quraysh were saying: 'Muhammad and his companions have violated the sacred month; they have shed blood in it, and taken booty, and captured prisoners.' The Jews interpreted the event as a bad omen for the apostle.

When speculation on the subject became widespread Allah revealed these words to His apostle: 'They will ask thee about the sacred month and the fighting. Say "To fight in the sacred month is a matter of grave import, but to obstruct the worship of Allah and not to believe in Him, to prevent men from entering the holy mosque or to drive them out of it, these are of even graver import." '

So the apostle of Allah took possession of the caravan and the prisoners. The Quraysh sent men to negotiate for the ransom of the prisoners, but the apostle replied that he could not release them until the two Emigrants who had fallen behind Abdullah to look for their camel returned, because he feared the Quraysh might have met and harmed them. 'If you have killed them, we shall kill our prisoners,' he said. But the two wanderers returned and the apostle released the prisoners, one of them making profession of Islam and remaining in Medina with Muhammad.

When Allah made plunder permissible He allowed four parts to those who had won it, and one part to Himself and to His apostle, exactly as Abdullah had done with the captured caravan.

This was the occasion when the first booty was taken by the Muslims, when the first prisoners were taken by the Muslims and when the first man was slain by the Muslims. It was eighteen months since the Emigrants had arrived in Medina.

Soon the apostle of Allah heard that Abu Sufyan – whom he had missed at al-Ushayra – was returning from Syria with a large caravan of merchandise, accompanied by thirty or forty men. Then he addressed the Believers, saying: 'Go forth against this caravan; it may be that Allah will grant you plunder.' The people soon assembled, though some were fearful and others hesitated because they had not thought the apostle would really go to war.

Meanwhile, Abu Sufyan was approaching the Hijaz, gathering information and questioning every rider he met, lest he expose his people to danger. At last he heard: 'Muhammad has gathered his companions to attack you and your caravan.' Greatly alarmed, he sent off a messenger named Damdam to Mecca to call out the Quraysh to protect their goods and to warn them of the threat of Muhammad and his companions.

When Damdam arrived in Mecca he cut off the nose of his camel, turned its saddle back to front, and rent his own shirt, all to indicate the alarming news he brought. He shouted, 'O, ye Quraysh! Your prized caravan is in danger from Muhammad. You may be too late to save it. Help! Go now!' The people hastened to prepare, exclaiming, 'Does Muhammad believe this will be as easy a victory as at Nakhla? No, this time we shall teach him otherwise!' Thus the Quraysh assembled, and not a well-born man among them remained behind save Abu Lahab, who sent in his place a man who owed him money and who could not pay.

The apostle himself left Medina with his companions early in the month of Ramadan [December], leaving Abu Lubaba in control of affairs at Medina.

The white banner of the apostle was carried by Musab, and one black banner (The Eagle) by Ali, and another by the Helpers. There were seventy camels, which the men rode in turn. When the party arrived in al-Safra, a village between two mountains, the apostle asked the names of the village tribes and was told they were called Banu al-Nar [sons of fire] and Banu Huraq [sons of burning]. The apostle was uneasy and read an evil omen in the names, so he by-passed the village and the mountains and travelled through a valley known as Dhafiran. Halting here, he received news that the Quraysh were on the march from Mecca to protect their caravan. He asked his people what they thought should be done and al-Miqdad said, 'Go where Allah leads! We are with thee, and we shall not say to thee what the children of Israel said to Moses, "Thou and thy Lord may go and fight; we shall remain here!" Instead we say "Go thou and thy Lord and fight; we shall fight with you!" ' The apostle thanked him for this declaration and blessed him, and said, 'Advise me also, you men of the Helpers.' He feared the Helpers might aid him only by defending him against attack in Medina, and that they would not think it incumbent upon them to fight for him outside their own territory. But Sad answered, 'We believe in thee, and have testified that the revelation thou hast brought is true. Therefore we have made a covenant! We hear and obey thee! Go where thou wilt, we are with thee; we shall be steady in battle and true in combat. And perhaps Allah will show thee something of us which will rejoice the eye, and procure the blessing of Allah.'

When the apostle of Allah arrived near Badr he received news of the whereabouts of the Quraysh, and sent several of his companions to the well at Badr to investigate further. The companions brought back two slaves, watermen of the Quraysh, who confessed to Muhammad that 'The Quraysh are at the rear of that sandhill.' The apostle asked, 'How many men are there?' and they replied, 'Many!' He asked, 'What is their number?' but the slaves said that they did not know. 'How many camels do they slaughter daily?' The slaves replied, 'Some days nine, and some days ten', and the apostle said, 'Then they must be from nine hundred to one thousand in number.'

Meanwhile, two of the companions had gone back to the well to fetch water, and they overheard a conversation between two girls and a tribesman, who said, 'Tomorrow or the day after tomorrow the caravan will arrive.'

Abu Sufyan, however, had scouted ahead of his caravan and he reached the water unobserved, after the two companions had left. There he asked the tribesman if any strangers had been seen and was told, 'No one suspicious, except two riders, who alighted near the hill, took water to fill their water-bottles and departed.' Abu Sufyan went to the spot where they had halted and, examining the camel-dung there, found that it contained date-stones. 'This is the fodder of Medina,' he exclaimed, and returning briskly to the caravan he diverted it from the road and along the coast, and by-passed Badr altogether. They hastened on beyond the reach of danger and when Abu Sufyan decided the caravan had reached safety he sent a message to the Quraysh army telling them they could return to Mecca.

But Abu Jahl refused to return to Mecca without giving a display of strength at Badr. 'We shall stay there three days, slaughter cattle, feast the people, drink wine, and be entertained by singing-girls. All Arabia will hear of us, of our march, of our festivity, and they will respect us ever afterwards! Therefore, let us proceed.' One group, who saw no further purpose in the expedition, returned to Mecca, but the rest of the army followed Abu Jahl.

The Quraysh army marched until they reached the sandy foothills on the western side of the valley of Badr, but they were impeded by rain and mud sent by Allah. In the valley itself Muhammad and his force were not so hampered, and they reached the wells of Badr first and halted at the nearest of them. Al-Hubab inquired of the apostle if this halting-place were the choice of Allah, and when the apostle replied that it had been selected according to his own strategy and according to no higher instruction, al-Hubab said: 'Then let the people arise and march to the well next to the enemy; on the way, let us close up all the wells except the last. Around that, let us make a reservoir and fill it with water; then, when we fight, we shall drink, but not the enemy.' The apostle replied, 'Thy advice is good!' and they acted accordingly.

Some of the Quraysh, however, went down to the reservoir and the apostle said, 'Let them drink', but only one man of those who drank survived the next day's battle. This was Hakim, who later professed Islam.

That night the Quraysh sent Umayr to spy out the number of the companions. He circled the army, then returned to report: 'They are a little more or less than three hundred in number; but give me time to see whether they have any other men in ambush or in reserve.' He again departed, and rode some distance, but returned and said, 'I have not seen anything; but listen to me. Battles bring misfortune. The camels of Medina carry sudden death. These men have no other refuge or protection than their swords and I believe that not one of them will die without first killing one of us. If one of us dies for every one of them, what will life have to offer after that?'

Then Utba rose and addressed the Quraysh: 'You will gain nothing by attacking Muhammad and his companions! If you conquer him, many of his men being our kinsmen, you will never escape the loathing of those fellow Quraysh whose kinsmen you have slain. Return therefore, and let Muhammad fight with other Arabs.' But Abu Jahl sneered, 'His lungs are swollen with fear at the sight of Muhammad and his companions! We shall not retreat until Allah decides between us and Muhammad', and he sent a message to Amir, the man whose brother had been killed at Nakhla, the first man killed in Islam. 'Your ally wishes to turn back. Arise, therefore, and avenge the murder of your brother by leading the people on to fight.' Thus the flame of war was fanned, the Quraysh became fixed in their evil course, and the advice of Utba was spurned.

When Utba heard of Abu Jahl's insult he cried, 'We shall see which of us two is the coward!' and sought a helmet to put on his head; but he could not find one in the whole army to fit because his skull was so great. So he wrapped a piece of cloth around his head.

Soon the apostle of Allah saw the Quraysh entering the valley, and he prayed. 'Allah! These are the Quraysh with their arrogance and vanity, who have offended Thee and accused Thy apostle of falsehood. O Allah! Grant me Thy promised aid and annihilate them this day!'

The battle of Badr took place on Friday morning, the seventeenth day of Ramadan.

One man of the Quraysh, a vicious, quarrelsome fellow, now stepped forth from the army and said, 'I call Allah as witness that I shall drink from their reservoir and destroy it, or die in the attempt.' Hamza advanced to do battle with him and when they met Hamza struck him violently and severed his leg between the knee and the foot. The man fell on his back and the blood from his leg spurted towards the Quraysh army; but he dragged himself on to the reservoir to redeem his vow. Hamza slew him there.

Next, Utba came forth, flanked by his brother and his son, and uttered the challenge to single combat. Three men of the Helpers stepped forward, but the Quraysh refused to fight with them and cried: 'Let us fight with equals from our own tribe!' So the apostle of Allah gave them Ubayda and Hamza and Ali, and they said, 'Agreed. These are noble and our equals!' Ubayda confronted Utba, Hamza confronted the brother of Utba, and Ali the son. Ubayda and Utba wounded one another, but Hamza and Ali killed their opponents at once and then turned and slew the wounded Utba. Thereafter, they carried Ubayda back to his companions.

The apostle of Allah took up a handful of gravel, and threw it in the direction of the Quraysh. 'May confusion strike them!' he cried, and ordered his companions to attack.

Victory was theirs, and Allah slew many of the Quraysh chiefs, and caused many of their nobles to be taken prisoner. According to one of Muhammad's followers, on the day of Badr one Abu Daud 'followed an idolater in order to strike him down, and lo! his head fell off ere my sabre reached it; then I knew that some other agency had killed him'. Turbans are the diadems of the Arabs, and the sign of the angels on that day was white turbans, flowing at the back; only Gabriel wore a yellow turban. The angels never fought with distinguishing marks except on the day of Badr. They were present at other battles, but merely to increase the numbers, not to fight.

Ukkasha fought on the day of Badr until his sword broke in his hand. Then the apostle went to him and gave him a piece of wood, saying, 'Fight with this'. When he took it in his hand and waved it, it became a sword with a long blade, strong, gleaming and sharp. He fought with it until Allah bestowed victory upon the Muslims that day, and kept it, and fought many battles with it in the company of the apostle of Allah.

As the companions were engaged in taking captives after the battle, the apostle of Allah saw signs of displeasure on the face of Sad, who stood beside him. The apostle said: 'You seem displeased with what the people are doing?' and Sad replied, 'Yes, by Allah. This is the first defeat which Allah has visited on the infidels, and I would rather have seen wholesale slaughter than this preservation of life.' The apostle of Allah, however, had told his companions that day: 'I know for a certainty that many of the Banu Hashim and others of the Quraysh have been brought against their will to fight us. If, therefore, any man of you meets one of the Banu Hashim he is not to kill him.' The apostle gave similar instructions concerning his uncle al-Abbas and certain others of the Quraysh who had protected the apostle in the past. Nevertheless, the slaughter was great.

On the day of Badr, after the battle, Abdul-Rahman passed near some Quraysh who had been unable to flee, and saw his old friend Ummaya with his son. Ummaya exclaimed: 'Are you willing to take me prisoner? My ransom will be of more value to you than the plunder you are laden with!' Throwing away his plunder, Abdul-Rahman took him and his son by the hand and walked with them. 'But Bilal saw him with me, and it was Ummaya who had tormented Bilal when he was a slave at Mecca. When he caught sight of him now, he exclaimed, "Worst of infidels! Let me die if he be allowed to live!" and he cried out to the companions of the apostle to kill Ummaya. They formed a ring round us, and I tried to protect him, but a man struck off the leg of the son of Ummaya and he fell to the ground. Then Ummaya uttered a cry such as I had never heard before. I said to him, 'Save thyself. I can no longer help thee,' and the people fell upon them with their swords and killed them both; and I said "May Allah have mercy on Bilal! My plunder has gone and he has deprived me of my captives, too!" '

After the apostle of Allah had done with the enemy, he ordered that the body of Abu Jahl be sought among the slain. The first man who had encountered Abu Jahl in the battle was Muadh, who had attacked him, and struck off his foot and ankle; but Abu Jahl's son dealt Muadh such a blow as almost cut his hand from his arm. 'It remained dangling at my side held only by the skin,' said Muadh. 'After that the battle drew me away from Abu Jahl and I continued to fight all day, dragging my hand after me; but after a while it annoyed me too much, and I placed my foot on it and wrenched it off. Then I threw it away.' Another of the companions later smote the crippled Abu Jahl, but there still remained a spark of life in him. When Muhammad ordered the search he was found by Abdullah b. Masud. 'I found him in his last agony and recognized him. I placed my foot on his neck – for he had once caught hold of me in Mecca, insulted me, and kicked me in the chest – and said to him "Allah has at last put you to shame, o enemy of Allah!" He retorted, "In what way has He put me to shame? Is it shame to a man that you have killed him? Tell me who is victorious this day?" I replied, "Allah and His apostle!" Then I cut off his head and brought it to the apostle of Allah and said, "This is the head of Abu Jahl, the enemy of Allah!" Then I threw the head down before the apostle, and he praised Allah.'

Then the apostle of Allah ordered the slain to be thrown into a pit and all were thrown into it, except Ummaya, whose body was so swollen that it could not easily be taken out of its armour; therefore they threw as much earth and rubble on the body as would cover it. When the bodies had been thrown into the pit the apostle said, 'Now, you people of the pit, have you realized the truth of your Lord's promise? For I have found what my Lord promised me has been fulfilled.' His companions said: 'Do you speak to dead men?' and he replied, 'They know that what I say is true!'

After the battle the apostle ordered all the plunder to be collected, and the companions disputed about it. Those who had collected it said, 'It belongs to us', and those who had pursued the enemy said, 'Had it not been for us, you would not have been able to collect it.' Those, too, who had guarded the person of the apostle lest he be attacked, said, 'You have no greater right to it than we. We desired to fight, but we could not leave the apostle of Allah.' Then Allah took out of their hands all cause for dispute, entrusting His apostle with the distribution of the spoils; and he promised equal shares to all the Muslims.

The apostle of Allah sent a messenger ahead to bear the glad tidings of victory, and then set off himself for Medina, with the army, plunder, and prisoners. At Rauha, the faithful met to congratulate him on the victory which Allah had granted to him and his companions. But Salama exclaimed: 'Why do you congratulate us? By Allah, we met only bald-headed old men whom we slaughtered like hobbled camels!' At this the apostle smiled and said, 'But, nephew, those were the elders of the community!'

At al-Safra, on the return journey, the apostle ordered one of the prisoners, al-Nadr, to be executed, and another, Uqba, later in the journey. The apostle of Allah reached Medina one day ahead of the prisoners, and when they arrived he distributed them among his companions, saying, 'Treat the captives well.' And they treated them with great kindliness.

Soon after his return the apostle assembled the Jews in the market-place and addressed them: 'Make profession of Islam before Allah punishes you as He has punished the Quraysh!' But they replied: 'Do not deceive yourself! You have slain a few Quraysh who were inexperienced and did not know how to fight. If you had fought with us, you would have learnt that we are men, such as whom you have not yet encountered.' Then Allah sent down the verse, 'Say to those who disbelieve, "You will be conquered and gathered together in hell. It was a miracle when the two armies met at Badr. One army fought in the name of Allah; the other was thrice their number but thought the Believers as numerous as themselves. But Allah gives strength by His aid to those whom He will." Surely in that there is a lesson for those with eyes to see'.

Concerning the affair of Badr, Allah revealed a whole Sura, *The Spoils*. 'Say "The spoils belong to Allah and to His apostle . . . Allah promised that one of the two parties [the caravan, or the Quraysh army] would fall to you, and some hoped that it might be the weaker one [the caravan]; but Allah proposed to establish the truth of His word, and to cut down the uttermost part of the Unbelievers. When you prayed for assistance from your Lord, beholding the multitude of your enemies, Allah said, 'I shall aid you with a thousand angels in serried ranks.' . . . And Allah instructed His angels, 'I shall throw terror into the hearts of those who disbelieve. Therefore strike off their heads and strike off their fingers, because they have resisted Allah and His apostle and Allah is severe in His punishment.'

' ". . . Those who *feign* belief in Allah are dumb concerning whatever is good, and deaf concerning the truth. If Allah knew there to be any good in them He would make their feigned belief into reality. If these Hypocrites had gone forth to battle with you, they would have turned back and failed you.

' "Ye who believe! Remember when you were few and weak

in the land, dreading the threat of being despoiled, He sheltered you, strengthened you with His aid, and provided you with good things, that you might be thankful. . . . Fear Allah! He will grant you deliverance, and will expiate your sins, and will forgive you; for Allah is generous. . . . And if those who disbelieve give up their disbelief, what is past shall be forgiven them, but if they come to attack you, they shall fare like those slain on the day of Badr. Therefore fight them, till there be no more persecution and all belong to Allah alone. Allah is your guardian and He is the best guardian and the best helper.

' ". . . Whenever you win plunder, a fifth shall belong to Allah and His apostle, and his kindred, and orphans, and the poor, and the traveller.

' ". . . When you meet an army in battle, stand firm and remember Allah, that you may prosper; and do not quarrel, lest My cause should suffer. Be not like those who make parade of their deeds in pursuit of the approbation of men, but act purely for the sake of Allah and for His reward in giving your religion victory; work only for this, and covet nothing else. . . . Prepare against the infidels what force you are able, that you may strike terror into your enemy and that of Allah. And whatever you shall expend for the religion of Allah, it shall be repaid unto you, and you shall not be without reward. But if they incline to peace, do you also incline to peace; and trust in Allah, for He heareth and knoweth all things.

' ". . . O, apostle of Allah! Stir up the Faithful to war; if twenty of you persevere, they shall overcome two hundred, and if there be one hundred of you, they shall overcome a thousand of those who disbelieve because they are a people who are not inspired." '

When this verse was revealed the Muslims thought it very hard and difficult that twenty of them should fight against two hundred, and one hundred against one thousand; so Allah eased the burden and replaced that verse with another: 'Now Allah hath eased you, for He knew you were weak. If there be one hundred of you who persevere, they shall overcome two hundred by the permission of Allah; and if you be one thousand, you shall overcome two thousand.' That is to say, they were to fight if the enemy outnumbered them by two to one, but they were permitted to retreat from any more uneven contest.

Allah said, 'You have sought ransoms and worldly goods, but Allah wants the next world', meaning that they should kill to spread His religion, which is the path to the next world. Allah had before this time determined not to mete out punishment save when His prohibitions were disregarded; otherwise the men of Badr would have been punished severely for taking captives. However, He allowed the spoils of war to the apostle and his companions as a gift from Allah the merciful, the compassionate. He said, 'Enjoy therefore what you have acquired, for it is lawful and good; and fear Allah, for Allah is forgiving and merciful.'

Then He called the Muslims to unite and made the Helpers and the Emigrants friends in religion, and declared infidels of all creeds to be alike excluded from the friendship of Muslims. 'Unless you do this, there will be doubt on earth and great corruption.'

In all, eighty-three Emigrants and two hundred and thirty-one Helpers took part in the battle of Badr, and eight of these died as martyrs in the fighting. Fifty Quraysh were slain and forty-three were made prisoner.

The battle of Badr was a turning-point in the history of Islam and 'the Three Hundred' who fought there became the most honoured of Believers. The apostle made full use of the divine intervention which had made such a victory possible, and the victory itself has been transmitted through the centuries in exhaustive detail. Badr also made total conflict with the people of Mecca inevitable: their honour had been brutally sullied by an outcast, and, furthermore, it was now clear that Muhammad intended to wrest from them the spiritual and temporal influence they had for so long wielded in the Arabian peninsula. The Quraysh had no alternative but to carry matters to a conclusion.

In Medina itself the apostle continued to be harassed by both Jews and Hypocrites. Not yet strong enough to take action against

*them as groups, he resorted to other tactics. The months following
Badr are marred by increasing ruthlessness and fanaticism, and by
murders carried out in a spirit of impassioned and bloody righteousness. The year after Badr passed in an atmosphere of excitable
unrest, and then came the salutary battle of Uhud.*

During the year which followed the battle of Badr the apostle
made several small raids on the Quraysh; while at Mecca those
sons whose fathers had been slain as Unbelievers at Badr
gathered their people together to fight the apostle. And they sent
their emissaries out into the countryside to stir up the people
against him.

At last the Quraysh marched out with the flower of their army,
with some black Abyssinian troops, with allies from the Banu
Kinana and the lowlands, and with women in howdahs who
went to keep their anger and courage alight. The army was led
by Abu Sufyan, and they went as far as Aynayn and halted on a
hill in the valley of Qanat near Medina.

When the apostle of Allah heard of this he said, 'By Allah, I
have had a favourable vision. I have seen cows, and a notch on
the blade of my sword; and in the vision I thrust my hand into a
strong coat of mail which represents, I believe, Medina.' Then
he told his followers, 'If you think it proper to remain in Medina
and leave the enemy where they are, it will be well; for they will
either remain in their position, which is a bad one, or come in to
us and we shall fight them in the town.' Although the apostle did
not wish to march out against the Unbelievers, several of his
followers – whom Allah favoured with a martyr's death on the
day of Uhud, and who included some who had missed the battle
at Badr – exclaimed, 'Come out with us against these enemies
lest they take us for cowards and weaklings.' Others said,
'Remain in Medina. Do not go out to them. If they enter Medina,
our men will fight them face to face, whilst our women and
children throw stones upon them from above; and, if they retreat,
they will retreat as disgraced as they came.' But the people who
wished to rush out and meet the enemy did not cease to importune the apostle of Allah until he entered his house and donned

his armour. All this took place on a Friday, when he had finished prayers.

When the apostle reappeared from his house, however, they had repented, and said, 'We have vexed thee, and ought not to have done so. Remain in the city, therefore, and may Allah bless thee!' But the apostle replied, 'After a prophet has put on his armour, he must not lay it aside until he has fought!' Therefore he marched out with seven hundred of his companions.

They advanced as far as the hollow of Uhud and the apostle said, 'Let no man of you fight until we command him.' Then he drew up his army in battle array and appointed over his fifty archers a man who was conspicuous by his white garb, saying to him, 'Keep off the cavalry with thy arrows, that they may not attack us from the rear. Whether the battle move in our favour or against us, always remain in thy place lest we be attacked from thy side.' Then the apostle of Allah put on two coats of mail and gave the standard to Musab.

The apostle offered a sword to his followers, saying, 'Who will take this sword for a worthy price?' Many coveted it, but he would not give it up until Abu Dujana asked, 'What is its price?' He replied, 'That thou strike the enemy with it until it bends', and Abu Dujana took the sword; he was a brave man, anxious to distinguish himself in war, and he was best known by his red head-dress which he wore when he was ready to fight. He took the sword, put on his red turban, and strutted about the ranks; seeing this, the apostle said, 'Such a gait pleases Allah only on occasions like this!'

The Quraysh also drew up in battle array; their army consisted of three thousand men including two hundred horsemen on the flanks, commanded by Khalid b. al-Walid on the right and by the son of Abu Jahl on the left.

As the two armies approached each other, Hind – the daughter of that Utba who had been slain at Badr – and the other women from Mecca beat their drums and uttered cries of encouragement to the Quraysh army.

On the day of Badr, the followers of the apostle had cried,

'One god! One god!' but on the day of Uhud their war cry was 'Slay! Slay!'

The people fought violently, and Abu Dujana penetrated into the very heart of the enemy army and killed every man he attacked. But there was one man among the Quraysh who never failed to kill any man he wounded, and these two met and exchanged blows. Then a blow from the infidel struck the shield of Abu Dujana and stuck there and Abu Dujana slew the man with a single blow. Soon he saw a Meccan inciting the enemy to further efforts and 'lifting my sword I heard a yell, and lo! It was a woman! [Hind.] I had too much respect for the sword of the apostle to kill a woman with it.'

Hamza also fought valiantly on that day, killing several infidels. But one of the Quraysh had instructed his slave Wahshi, who was an Abyssinian and skilled in throwing the javelin, that he must kill Hamza in the battle. 'If you kill Hamza, the uncle of Muhammad, in revenge for my uncle who died at Badr, you will be free.' While Hamza was engaged in battle with another man, Wahshi related, 'I poised my spear well and threw it with such force at his groin that it came out between his legs at the back. He was overcome with weakness and fell, and I waited until he expired then went and took out my spear from his body. Then I returned proudly to the camp, for I had business with no other but him.'

Musab, too, died on that day, being slain by one who mistook him for the apostle of Allah and returned to his army, saying, 'I have killed Muhammad.' When Musab was slain, the apostle gave the banner to Ali, and Ali and the Muslims continued to fight.

Then Allah sent his aid to the Muslims and fulfilled his promise so that they assailed the infidels with their swords and put them to flight. But the Muslim archers disobeyed the orders of the apostle and turned aside into the deserted Quraysh camp, leaving the Believers' rear open to the Quraysh cavalry. And the Quraysh cavalry attacked and put the Muslims to flight.

Soon the enemy even approached the apostle himself. He was struck down by stones and one of his front teeth was lost.

'His face being wounded, blood trickled down it; and wiping it, he exclaimed: "How can a nation prosper which dyes the face of its prophet with blood, though he invites them to the worship of Allah?" ' Ali took the apostle by the hand, and Talha lifted him up until he stood upright; Malik licked the blood from the face of the apostle and swallowed it, and the apostle said, 'He whose blood has touched mine will be exempted from the threat of hell-fire.' When the foe pressed close on the apostle, he asked, 'Who will save my life?' and six men of his followers arose and fought by his side. One by one they were martyred until a single defender remained, and he, too, was wounded; but a company of Muslims arrived and put the infidels to flight. Then the apostle said 'Bring him near to me!' and they brought the wounded man to him and he made his foot a pillow under the man's head; and thus he expired, with his cheek on the foot of the apostle of Allah.

Abu Dujana now shielded the apostle with his body, bending over him so that his own back would accept the thickly falling arrows of the enemy, and Sad, nearby, shot at the infidels with the apostle 'handing arrows to me, saying "Shoot. May my father and mother be a ransom for thee!" He even gave me an arrow without a point, saying "Shoot with that!" ' The apostle of Allah also shot arrows himself until his bow broke. The bow was then taken and prized by Qata, whose eye was injured on that day so that it hung out upon his cheek; but the apostle of Allah replaced the eye in its socket with his own hand, and afterwards it became the better, and the keener of his two eyes.

The first man who recognized the apostle of Allah after the rumour spread that he had been killed, was Kab; 'I recognized his eyes under the helmet, and I shouted with my loudest voice "O Muslims, rejoice! Here is the apostle of Allah!" But he beckoned to me to remain quiet.'

Now the apostle, with Abu Bakr, Umar, Ali, Talha, al-Zubayr and others withdrew to a hollow near by, and rested.

Ali went out and filled his water-bottle from the reservoir, and brought it to the apostle to drink from; but he found it had an evil smell, and would not drink. Instead he washed the blood from his face, and as he did so, said, 'The wrath of Allah will be great against him who made the face of His prophet bleed.' While the apostle and his companions were in the hollow, the Quraysh cavalry appeared on the mountain, and the apostle exclaimed, 'O Allah! it is not meet that they should be above us!' So a company of the Emigrants attacked them and drove them off; but most of the apostle's army had fled.

The infidel woman, Hind, and her companions mutilated the bodies of the Muslims slain that day; they cut off the ears and noses, and Hind made necklaces, bracelets and earrings from them. Also she cut off a piece of Hamza's liver and chewed it but could not swallow it, so she spat it out again. Then she climbed a high rock and shouted the Quraysh victory from it.

When Abu Sufyan decided to leave the field of battle, he climbed to the mountain and cried aloud, 'The day is decided; victory goes by turns – today in exchange for the day of Badr! Defend thy religion!' The apostle said to Umar, 'Arise and say "Allah is the most high and glorious. Our slain are in paradise; yours are in hell." ' After Umar had exposed himself and replied thus, Abu Sufyan summoned him to approach and asked, 'Have we killed Muhammad?' Umar replied, 'No, praise be to Allah. He hears your words.' Then Abu Sufyan shouted, 'Some of your dead have been mutilated, but I am neither pleased nor displeased, I neither forbade it nor commanded it. We shall meet at Badr next year'; and he and his companions prepared to depart. The apostle of Allah instructed one of his companions to reply, 'Agreed. Let that be our meeting-place.'

Then the people of Medina went searching for their dead, and the apostle sent a man of the Helpers to see whether Sad were alive or dead; the man found Sad fatally wounded. 'I am among the dead,' he said. 'Give my salutations to my people and say I sent them this message: "There will be no forgiveness from Allah for you if your prophet is injured as long as you have life in you." ' Thus saying, he died. The apostle himself went out in search of his uncle, Hamza, and when he found the mangled body he said, 'If it were not that it would pain his sister and that it might become customary after me, I would leave this body to be consumed by the beasts and birds. But if Allah aids me against the Quraysh in a future battle, I shall mutilate thirty men of them.' When the Muslims saw the apostle's grief and his wrath against those who had dealt thus with his uncle they swore that if Allah should aid them to victory they would mutilate their foes as no Arab had been mutilated before. But Allah sent down a commandment, and his apostle followed it by giving pardon, waiting in patience, and forbidding mutilation. The other corpses were placed by the side of Hamza, and seventy-two prayers were spoken over them, and then they were interred.

The apostle returned to Medina and there was great lamentation there. He passed a house of the Helpers and heard weeping for the dead, and his own eyes overflowed with tears as he realized that there were no women to weep for Hamza. Then two of his companions returned and ordered their women to gird up their loins and go weep for the uncle of the apostle. The apostle listened and then went out to them, saying, 'Return home, and Allah have mercy upon you. You exhaust yourselves.' On that day the apostle prohibited wailing and lamentation.

One woman lost her husband, her brother and her father on that day of Uhud, but when she was told of their deaths she asked, 'What of the apostle of Allah?' They replied, 'He is well', and she said, 'If he is still with us, all other misfortunes are trifling.'

When the apostle arrived at the home of his family he gave his sword to his daughter Fatima, saying, 'Wash the blood from it, little one. By Allah, it has been true to me today.' Ali, too, gave her his sword and said, 'Take this and wash the blood from it. By Allah, it has been true to me today'. The name of the apostle's sword was Dhul-Faqar.

The next morning, so that the enemy might know they were pursued and that the followers of the apostle were in no way cowed by the result of the battle of Uhud, Muhammad and the survivors marched out for eight miles from the city, as far as Hamraul-Asad and remained there three days before returning to Medina.

The day of Uhud was a day of testing, of calamity and of purification, when Allah put the Faithful on trial and struck at those whose belief was no deeper than their words; it was a day on which Allah rewarded those he designed to favour with the reward of martyrdom.

The part of the Koran revealed by Allah concerning the day of Uhud amounts to sixty verses of the Sura, *Family of Imran*. It mentions the calamity which befell the Faithful at Uhud, and the trial which led to their purification and His taking martyrs from among them. Then Allah gave them consolation and information: 'Before your time, there have been examples set; go over the earth and behold what has become of those who accused the apostle of Allah of imposture. . . . This is a clear declaration to men and an admonition to the pious. Be not dismayed or grieved over what has befallen, for you shall enjoy the end and the victory if you are Believers. If a hurt has been inflicted upon you, your enemies have received as great a hurt, and we cause such days to alternate among men that Allah may know those who believe and may take martyrs from among you; Allah loveth not those whose belief is in their mouth and not in their heart. . . . Did you imagine you should enter paradise when Allah as yet knew not which among you was strong to fight, and steadfast?

'. . . Allah had already made good unto you His promise [at Uhud] and you put the infidels to flight by His permission; but you became faint-hearted and disputed about His command and disobeyed His prophet [when the archers went after plunder instead of keeping their position]. So He made you flee from them to try you. But now He hath pardoned you, for He is generous towards the Faithful. Do not believe that the infidels will be victorious in the end, but hold fast to Me and obey My command. . . . Trust in Allah, for Allah loveth those who trust in Him. If Allah aid you, none shall conquer you, but if He desert you, who will aid you? . . . Allah was gracious unto the Believers when He raised up among them an apostle of their own nation who should recite His signs unto them and purify them and teach them the scripture and wisdom; whereas they were before in manifest error. When a misfortune befalls you [at Uhud] after you have won a battle twice as great, do not say "Whence cometh this?" Say "This is from ourselves, because Allah is omnipotent." And what happened to you on the day when the two armies met was by the permission of Allah, in order that He might know the Believers, and also the Hypocrites among you . . .

'Do not think that those slain in the path of Allah are dead; I have raised them up again and they are with Me, rejoicing in the pleasures and the cool breezes of paradise, happy in the reward Allah has bestowed upon them because they waged holy war for Him.'

Then the apostle said, 'When your brothers were defeated at Uhud, Allah placed their souls in the bodies of green birds, which flit about the rivers of paradise and drink the waters of the river and eat the fruits of the garden of paradise and perch on golden candlesticks under the throne of Allah. When they learned the pleasure of all this, they said, "Would that our brothers knew what Allah had given us, that they might not weaken in their efforts in the holy war." '

Of the Muslims who fought on the day of Uhud, sixty-five were martyred; and twenty-two infidels were slain on that day.

This explanatory – and, in its complete form, extremely lengthy – Sura from Allah was very necessary to restore the badly shaken faith of the Believers. The argument that Allah wished to discover the Hypocrites among the warriors lacked conviction in face of the fundamental tenet 'Allah knows all', but the failure of the archers to carry out their orders, thus turning victory into defeat, was much more plausible and confirmed the often-repeated injunction to obey 'Allah and His prophet'. The apostle soon restored his people to serenity, and the dead of Uhud became revered as martyrs.

After Uhud, in the third year of the Hijra, a deputation came from two neighbouring tribes who asked Muhammad to send teachers with them to instruct them in Islam. The apostle sent Marthad, Khalid, Asim, Khubayb, Zayd b. al-Dathinna, and Abdullah b. Tariq, and they went with the tribesmen as far as the water of al-Raji, which belonged to the Hudhayl tribe. Then the tribesmen betrayed them and men with swords fell upon them while they were resting in the night; but when the men from Medina snatched up their own swords, their attackers swore they did not wish to kill them, but only to make use of them in an attempt to gain something from the people of Mecca. Marthad, Khalid and Asim replied, 'By Allah! We never believe a promise or a covenant from an idolater', and they fought against the idolaters and were slain.

Asim had killed the two sons of a Meccan woman on the day of Uhud and she had sworn to have the skull of Asim and drink wine from it. But a swarm of bees settled around his body and kept the idolaters away; they said, 'Leave him there until the evening when the bees go away, and then we shall cut off his head.' But Allah sent a torrent of water and swept away the body of Asim, who had sworn to Him that he would never touch or be touched by an idolater lest he be defiled; thus Allah protected him from defilement after death as he had been protected in life.

The other three men from Medina surrendered themselves and were taken to Mecca to be sold, but Abdullah tried to escape on the way and was killed. Khubayb and Zayd were exchanged by their captors for two prisoners of their own tribe who were held by the Quraysh, and the Quraysh slew Zayd and crucified Khubayb in revenge for the deaths at Uhud.

Four months later a similar treachery took place. Forty of the best of the Muslims went out as invited guests to tell of Islam to the people of Najd and all save two were slain.

Shortly after this the Jews of the Banu al-Nadir plotted to murder the apostle of Allah himself, but Allah sent down a warning to the apostle. He issued orders to prepare an expedition against the Jews, and marched out and besieged them for six nights, during which time Allah sent down the prohibition against the drinking of wine.

Meanwhile, certain persons of Medina who were not Believers sent a message to the Banu al-Nadir, saying, 'Hold out, and defend yourselves; we shall not surrender you to Muhammad. If you are attacked we shall fight with you and if you are sent away we shall go with you.' But they were in truth unwilling to fight on behalf of the al-Nadir, for Allah had filled their hearts with terror. Then the Jewish tribe asked that the apostle of Allah should not shed their blood, but permit them to carry away as much of their property as their camels could bear. He consented and they loaded as many of their possessions as they could on their camels, even demolishing their houses that they might take away the thresholds. Then they left, with their wives, children, and household goods, and accompanied by their drums, flutes and singers. The rest they left to the apostle of Allah.

When the Jews had departed Muhammad went on an expedition to punish the people of Najd, who had slain all but two of the forty men he had sent to instruct the people in Islam. The parties approached each other, but no battle took place, for they were afraid of each other, and the apostle marched his men away again.

In the fourth year of the Hijra the apostle marched to Badr as he had agreed with Abu Sufyan after the battle of Uhud, and waited there eight days. Abu Sufyan marched out from Mecca with his army as far as Majanna; then he said to his people, 'This is not meet for you, save in a year of plenty when there are shrubs where the cattle may browse and milk for the men to drink. This year is one of scarcity and I shall return home. Do you likewise.' So the Quraysh army returned to Mecca and were nicknamed by the people who had stayed at home 'the Sawiq army' – the army that went out only to drink porridge. So Muhammad waited in vain at Badr and then returned to Medina.

For some months after 'the Second Badr', Muhammad was occupied in small punitive and foraging expeditions, during one of which he ventured as far as the borders of Syria.
His personal life at this time was not without incident. Since the death of Khadija, he had acquired seven wives, foremost among whom was the daughter of Abu Bakr, Aisha. She had been married to the apostle at the age of ten, and was still only sixteen years old when, quite innocently, she provoked a scandal at Medina.

According to Aisha, 'When the apostle of Allah was about to

THE LIFE OF MUHAMMAD

depart on a journey, he used to throw lots to decide which of his wives he would take with him. Before an expedition against the Banu Mustaliq, my lot came out; so the apostle of Allah took me with him. In those days women used to eat only the necessities of life, and did not become strong and heavy on meat. When my camel was ready, I would seat myself in the howdah, which my attendants would then lift on to the back of the camel; then they would attach it to the beast and we could set off.

'During our return from the Mustaliq expedition we paused to rest for a night. Before the company set off again, I withdrew for a moment; but I was wearing a string of Yemeni beads and when I returned I found they had fallen from my neck. Although the people were about to start I went back to the place where I had been and searched until I found them. The attendants who were in the habit of saddling my camel had meanwhile done so and had taken up the howdah (thinking that I was in it as usual) and tied it upon the camel; then they had led the camel off. When I returned to the camp not a soul was there, so I wrapped myself in my cloak and laid myself down, for I knew that they would miss me and come to seek me.

'While I was thus reclining, Sufwan – who had fallen behind the company for some reason, and had not spent the night with them – passed by and observed me. He exclaimed, "To Allah we belong, and to Him we must return! This is the wife of the apostle of Allah!" and he brought his camel near and said, "Mount!" He withdrew a little and I mounted, then he took hold of the camel's head and advanced rapidly, being anxious to overtake the company; but we neither overtook them, nor did they miss me, until they again encamped. When Sufwan arrived, leading me on his camel, slander was uttered against me although I knew nothing of it.

'I became very ill when we arrived in Medina and so I still did not hear the slanders, but they were communicated to the apostle as well as to my parents. They did not speak of it to me, but I observed the absence of that kindliness which the apostle of Allah used always to show me when I was ill. This I thought strange on his part. However, I knew nothing of the matter until I had recovered from my illness, after more than twenty days.

'At that time we still lived like true Arabs and had no privies in our houses as the Persians did, because we despised and disliked such luxuries. Instead, we went out to an open plain in Medina, the women going at night. Thus I walked out one night, and the woman who walked with me stumbled over the hem of her skirt and cursed, saying "Let Auf perish!" "By Allah!" I exclaimed. "That seems to me an evil wish, since it concerns a Believer who has fought at Badr." The woman asked, "Has not the news reached thee, o daughter of Abu Bakr?" and when I asked what news she told me of the slanders. I could scarce believe it and fled to the house of my mother, weeping so that I thought my heart would break. I said to my mother, "May Allah forgive thee; the people slander me and you have said nothing of it to me!" and she replied, "Do not be unhappy. There are but few handsome women – who are loved by their husbands, and have rivals – who escape false imputations and slander."

'Meanwhile, unknown to me, the apostle of Allah addressed the people, glorified and praised Allah, and said, "How do you dare to insult me by insulting my family, and by saying things about them which are not true? By Allah, I know nothing but good of them." [The lies were spread by some of the Khazraj and by the sister of another wife of the apostle.] When the apostle of Allah had finished, Usayd, one of the Aus, rose and said, "If the slanders are spoken by the Aus, we shall silence them; and if they be spoken by our brothers, the Khazraj, say the word and we shall punish them!" Then one Sad b. Ubada, who had hitherto seemed a true Believer, said, "You lie. By Allah, you have suggested this punishment only because you know the slanderers are of the Khazraj; had they been of your tribe you would not have suggested it." Usayd retorted, "*You* lie, by Allah! You are a Hypocrite and give your support to the Hypocrites!" Then the people assailed each other, and it would have taken little for evil to come to pass between the two tribes.

'The Apostle of Allah now consulted Ali and Usama, and

Usama spoke only what was good, saying, "O apostle of Allah. We know only good of Aisha, and thou knowest only good of her, and these are merely false and idle rumours!" But Ali said, "There are many women! Thou canst take another! Ask her slave and she will tell thee the truth." So the apostle of Allah summoned my slave to examine her. Ali rose and struck the woman a violent blow, and said, "Tell the truth to the apostle of Allah", and she replied, "I know only what is good; and I cannot say ill of Aisha, save that one day I was kneading my dough and asked her to watch it, but she fell asleep and a sheep came and ate it up."

'After this, the apostle came to me, while both my parents were with me; and I wept. He sat down, glorified and praised Allah, and then said, "Thou must have heard what the people are saying. Fear Allah! If thou hast done wrong, then repent, for Allah accepts the repentance of his servants." While he spoke thus, my tears ceased to flow. I waited for my parents to reply to the apostle, but neither of them spoke; and I entertained too low an opinion of myself to hope that Allah would reveal verses of the Koran about me. But I hoped the apostle might have a vision in his sleep, in which Allah would expose the liars, or justify me, or tell the apostle the truth. When I saw that my parents did not speak, I asked, "Will you not reply to the apostle of Allah?" They said, "We know not what to say to him!"

'When I saw my parents thus estranged from me my tears flowed once more, and I cried, "I shall never repent to Allah for what I am accused of, because Allah knoweth I should be repenting something which did not occur, and thus I should speak untruth. But if I deny the charges, you will not believe me."

'And the apostle of Allah had not yet left us when he lost consciousness, as always happened before a revelation; then I neither feared nor cared, for I knew that I was innocent, and that Allah would do no injustice to me. But my parents seemed about to die for fear, lest Allah might send a revelation confirming the words of the slanderers.

'The apostle of Allah came back to consciousness and sat up, and the perspiration trickled like pearls from his forehead, although it was a winter day. Then he wiped it away, and said, "Allah has revealed thy innocence", and I replied, "Allah be praised!" After that, he went out to the people and recited to them verses of the Koran revealed to him by Allah, and he ordered the slanderers to be scourged.'

Sufwan, who had been slandered with Aisha, met one of the worst slanderers, the poet Hassan, and struck him with his sword. Another man, Thabit, hastened to assist Hassan, grasping Sufwan, and tying his hands to his neck with a rope; he then took him to the dwelling of one of the Khazraj, where Abdullah b. Rawaha met them. He asked, 'What is this?' and Thabit replied, 'Are you displeased? He struck Hassan with a sword and, by Allah, he might have killed him.' Abdullah asked, 'Does the apostle of Allah know of this?' and when Thabit said he did not, Abdullah told him, 'You have been presumptuous! Let the man go.'

When the apostle heard of this, he had Sufwan and Hassan brought before him, and Sufwan explained, 'He offended and mocked me; anger overcame me, and I struck him.' Then the apostle said to Hassan, 'Why do you malign my people when Allah has given them enlightenment? I think you deserved the blow.' However, the apostle soothed the poet by presenting him with a fortress in Medina, and a Coptic slave girl. Then Hassan composed verses complimentary to the chastity and beauty of Aisha.

In the fifth year of the Hijra the campaign of the Ditch occurred. A number of Jews went to the Quraysh in Mecca and invited them to wage war against the apostle of Allah, saying, 'We shall aid you against him until we wipe out him and his followers.' The Quraysh replied, 'You are the possessors of the first scripture; tell us whether our religion is better than his?' They said, 'Your religion is better than his, and you are nearer to the truth than he.' Then the Quraysh were encouraged to accept the invitation to fight against the apostle of Allah, and the Jews went to the Ghatafan and invited them to wage war against the apostle of

Allah, saying they would aid them, and that the Quraysh had already consented to fight.

So the Quraysh marched out under the command of Abu Sufyan, and the Ghatafan under the command of Uyayna.

When the apostle of Allah heard of their intention he made a ditch around Medina, working there himself in order to encourage the Muslims to covet reward in paradise, and they worked diligently with him except for the Hypocrites among them, who were dilatory, pretended to be ill, and stole away to their families without the permission or knowledge of the apostle. Any true Muslim, faced by an unavoidable emergency, always reported it to the apostle of Allah and obtained his permission to attend to the business. And Allah, the most high and glorious, revealed the verse 'When Believers are engaged with the apostle in public business, they do not depart without asking his permission. For those who ask permission are those who believe in Allah and in His apostle. . . . But Allah knoweth those who steal away privately; let those who resist His command take heed, lest some calamity befall them, or grievous punishment.' So the Muslims worked in the ditch till they had fortified it.

While the ditch was being excavated, Allah caused certain things to happen to display the truth of His apostle and confirm his prophetic dignity. The hard soil which they met with in some parts of the trench distressed the Muslims, and they complained to the apostle, who asked for a vessel of water. He spat into it, prayed for a while according to the will of Allah, and then poured the water on the hard soil. Those who were present said, 'The soil softened till it became like a sand heap, and resisted neither pickaxe nor hoe.'

On another occasion a little girl was sent to take dates to her father and uncle for breakfast. 'I went, and while looking for my father and uncle I happened to pass near the apostle of Allah, who said, "Come here, my little one. What hast thou there?" I replied, "These are dates which my mother sends to my father and to my uncle for their breakfast." Then the apostle said, "Give them to me." So I poured them into the palms of his hands, and they did not overflow. He ordered a cloth to be spread out, and placed the dates on it, then he said to a man nearby, "Call the people of the Ditch to come to breakfast." The men arrived and began to eat of the dates, but they increased in such a manner that when the men of the Ditch went away the dates were still overflowing from the sides of the cloth.'

Another man told how 'We were working with the apostle in the Ditch, and I had with me a small lamb which was not very fat; and I said, "We might prepare it for the apostle of Allah." So I ordered my wife to grind some barley and to bake with it some bread; then I slaughtered the lamb, and we roasted it for the apostle. When the evening set in, and the apostle was about to depart from the Ditch (it being our custom to work there during the day and return to our families in the evening), I said, "Apostle of Allah! I have prepared for thee a young lamb, and we have baked some barley-bread; and I should be honoured if thou were to come with me to my house." I wanted him to come alone, but when I had uttered the words, he ordered a crier to shout, "Follow the apostle of Allah." Then I said to myself, "To Allah we belong and to Him we must return." The apostle came, and the people with him. He took his seat, we brought the roasted lamb, he pronounced grace in the name of Allah, ate, and the people did so, too, one after the other; and when they had finished they rose and another batch of men arrived, till all the people of the Ditch had been fed on my one lamb.'

Salman the Persian told how 'I was digging in a portion of the Ditch and found it hard. The apostle was near me, and when he saw how troublesome the spot was, he came down, took the pick-axe from my hand, and struck the soil thrice. And each stroke brought forth a spark. Then I said, "Thou art to me as my father and mother, o apostle of Allah! What was this lightning I saw under the pickaxe when thou struck the soil?" He asked, "Didst thou really see it, Salman?" and I said, "Yes." He told me, "The first spark means that Allah has promised me the conquest of Yemen; the second that Allah has granted me the conquest of Syria and the West; and the third that Allah has bestowed upon me victory over the East." '

When the apostle of Allah had completed the Ditch, the Quraysh came and encamped at the confluence of the Ruma torrents. Their army consisted of 10,000 men, including their allies and followers; the Ghatafan, with their followers from Najd, also came and encamped in the direction of Uhud; and news came that the Jewish tribe of Banu Qurayza had broken their treaty with Muhammad. So the apostle of Allah marched out with his Muslims, amounting to 3,000 men in all, and encamped so that Sal was behind him and the Ditch in front, separating him from the enemy. He had ordered the children and the women to be shut up in the forts.

To the followers of the apostle fear was in the air; the enemy was on all sides and the Believers gave way to every kind of surmise. The Hypocrisy of some became manifest, and one man even declared, 'Muhammad used to promise us that he would swallow the treasures of Croesus and of Caesar; but at this moment, no one of us can even feel safe when he goes to relieve himself!'

Then the apostle of Allah and the idolaters remained encamped more than twenty days opposite each other, without any hostilities taking place save for the shooting of arrows and the siege.

When the difficulties of the siege began to bear hard on the people the apostle of Allah dispatched messengers to two commanders of the Ghatafan, promising them one-third of the date-crop of Medina if they agreed to depart with their people, and to leave him alone with his. Peace was concluded between them to the extent of drafting a document; but the final signature brought hesitation. The apostle sent for two of his Believers and consulted them. They asked, 'Is this something *thou* wouldst wish to do? Or is it something which Allah has commanded thee, and which we must do? Or is it something which thou wouldst wish to do for our sake?' He replied, 'It is something which I wish to do for your sake; and by Allah, I would not do it but that the Arabs shoot at you as from one bow, and distress you from all sides. It is my intention to lessen their sting somewhat.' Then one of the men exclaimed, 'We and these people were once idolaters together, but they did not eat of our dates except as our guests or for money. Shall we now – when Allah has favoured us with Islam, and has honoured us with it and with thee – present them with our property? We shall not. By Allah, we shall not give them anything except the sword, until Allah decides between us and them.' The apostle said, 'You are right', and the man took the document and obliterated the writing, and he said, 'Let them do their worst against us!'

So the apostle and the Muslims held on and their enemies besieged them, but no battle took place except that some horsemen of the Quraysh rode out dressed for battle on their horses; and they cried to the defenders, 'Prepare for battle, and you shall know who are the true fighters this day!' Then they pranced around and came to a halt near the ditch. When they saw it, they said, 'This is a device which no Arab has thought of!' (Indeed, it is said that Salman the Persian suggested it to the apostle of Allah.) Then they sought out a narrow part of the ditch and whipped their horses across it and drew them up in the marshy area between the ditch and Mount Sal. Now Ali rushed out with several companions to guard the spot over which the horses had leapt, and the horsemen galloped up to them. Their leader gave the challenge to single combat which was accepted by Ali, and Ali slew him and the other horsemen fled back to their army.

Safiya, the daughter of Abdul-Muttalib, was at the fort of Hassan, who had remained to guard the women and children. She told how 'A Jew approached and began to walk round the fort. Now, the Banu Qurayza Jews had broken their treaty with the apostle of Allah, and their fort was to the rear of ours. There was no one to protect our side of the city, and the apostle of Allah was occupied with the invaders and unable to come to our aid. Accordingly, I said, "O Hassan! A Jew is walking round the fort, and by Allah! I am not convinced that he will not report our weak position to the Jews in our rear. The apostle is fully engaged; go thou therefore to the man and kill him." He replied, "May Allah pardon thee! Thou knowest full well that this is not a task for me." When I saw that he would do nothing, I girded my loins, took a stick, went down to the Jew and struck him so that I killed him. After that, I returned to the fort and said, "O Hassan! Go down and plunder him; all that hindered me from doing it was that he is a man." But he replied, "I have no need to plunder him." '

While the apostle and his army were suffering tribulation, Nuaym came to him and said, 'I have made profession of Islam, but my people do not know this. I am at your command.' The apostle replied, 'You are but one man, so aid us by any stratagem you can; war itself is a deception.'

Then Nuaym went out to the Banu Qurayza, whose companion he had been in the time of idolatry, and said to them, 'You know how much I love you, and how friendly we are.' They replied, 'We have no suspicions about you', and Nuaym continued, 'The Quraysh are not like you; this is your own country; your property, your wives, and your children are all here; you cannot exchange it for another. But the Quraysh and the Ghatafan have come from far away to fight Muhammad, and you are helping them against him. Their country and property are at a distance and, if they are successful, they will take advantage and plunder this region; but if they fail, they will return to their own country, and leave you to Muhammad's vengeance. Abstain, therefore, from fighting in support of these tribes, unless they give you hostages from among their nobles as a security that you will all fight against Muhammad until you have truly destroyed him.' They replied, 'That is sensible advice.'

After that, Nuaym went away and talked with the Quraysh. He said to Abu Sufyan, 'You know my liking for you, and that I am estranged from Muhammad. Some information has reached me which I think it my duty to tell you, but you must keep it secret.' He replied, 'We shall do so!' and Nuaym went on, 'The Jews have repented of acting against Muhammad; they sent him the following message: "We are indeed sorry for what we have done; would you like us to take from the Quraysh and from the Ghatafan some of their nobles, whom we shall surrender to you that you may strike off their heads? After that we shall aid you against the rest of them until we wipe them out." Muhammad has agreed to this; so if the Jews ask hostages from you, do not give them a single man.'

After this, Muaym went to the Ghatafan and said, 'You are of the same descent and clan as I; I love you more than any other race of men and I believe you have no reason to suspect me?' They replied, 'That is true.' 'Then keep my secret,' he said, and they agreed. Then he spoke to them as he had spoken to the Quraysh, and warned them in the same way.

On the Friday evening Abu Sufyan and the chiefs of the Ghatafan sent the son of Abu Jahl with several companions to see the Banu Qurayza, and to test them, saying, 'We have no permanent camp here and our camels and horses are dying. Therefore prepare to fight Muhammad on the morrow, and we may vanquish him, and make an end to the contest.' But the Qurayza said, 'Tomorrow is the Sabbath day, on which we do no work; some of us have broken it before, as you know, and have been punished. In any case, we do not intend to fight with you against Muhammad, unless you give us hostages as a security until we overcome Muhammad, because we suspect that, if the war begins to be too much for you, you will simply depart to your country and leave us to the mercy of Muhammad.' When the messengers returned with this answer, the Quraysh and the Ghatafan said, 'What Nuaym told us is true.' So they dispatched a reply to the Qurayza, saying, 'We shall not surrender one of our men to you, but if you desire to fight, come and fight.' When the messengers delivered this reply, the Qurayza also said, 'What Nuaym told us is true! These people are determined to fight and if they have an opportunity they will make use of it; otherwise, they will depart to their own country, and leave us to Muhammad.'

Thus Allah estranged them from each other. And He also sent a piercing wind against them in the cold winter nights, which overturned their cooking-pots and blew down their tents.

When it came to the knowledge of the apostle that his enemies disagreed, he called Hudhayfa and sent him to find out what was happening. Long after, Hudhayfa described that night. 'The apostle prayed for part of the night, then turned to us and said,

"Who will go and see what our enemy is doing? Whoever goes will have a safe return, and I shall pray to Allah to make him my companion in paradise." But not one of the people would rise, because of their great fear, their great hunger, and the great cold; and when no one rose the apostle of Allah called me and said, "Hudhayfa! Go forth, enter among the enemy and see what they are doing, then return to me." Then I went out and moved among the enemy, while the wind and the hosts of Allah so worked among them that neither a cooking-pot nor a fire nor a tent remained unharmed. And Abu Sufyan rose and said, "Let every man identify his neighbour!" Accordingly I took the hand of the man next to me and asked "Who are you?" and he told me his name. Abu Sufyan continued, "This is not our home. Our cattle and camels have perished, the Banu Qurayza have abandoned us and their attitude is disquieting. We suffer from this violent gale; not a cooking-pot is safe, nor a fire burning, nor a tent standing! Go, as I am going!" Then he went to his camel and mounted, and whipped it upright.

'Accordingly I went back to the apostle, whom I found praying, and told him my tidings.' In the morning, the Quraysh had vanished, and the Ghatafan, too. Then the apostle of Allah and his army left the Ditch and returned to Medina and put away their arms.

At noon of the same day Gabriel came to the apostle, wearing a silken turban and riding on a mule saddled with brocade. He said, 'Hast thou put away thy arms, apostle of Allah?' He replied, 'Yes', and Gabriel said, 'But the angels have not yet put away theirs. I have come here to call the people to follow the command of Allah and march against the Banu Qurayza. I go myself to make them tremble.' Therefore the apostle of Allah ordered it to be proclaimed that none should hold afternoon prayers until they reached the Jewish stronghold.

The apostle sent Ali ahead with his standard and the people hastened to join it. When Ali reached the fort he heard language offensive to Islam and returned to meet the apostle, whom he warned not to approach the Qurayza. 'Why?' asked the apostle.

'Didst thou hear them insult me? Had they seen *me* there, they would not have spoken thus.' When he arrived in the territory of Qurayza he alighted near the Well of Ana and the people assembled around him. Many arrived after the last evening prayers without having held their afternoon prayers, so they held their afternoon prayers after the last evening prayers; but Allah did not punish them for that nor did the apostle of Allah reproach them.

The apostle of Allah besieged the Qurayza for twenty-five days until they were distressed, and Allah struck fear into their hearts.

When they had become convinced that the apostle would not depart until he had humbled them, Kab, their chief, spoke to them thus. 'I have three suggestions to make, of which you may select whichever you prefer. We can obey this man and believe in him; for it is plain that he is an inspired prophet. In this case, your lives, property and children will be secure.' They replied, 'We shall never abandon the commandments of the Torah, nor substitute any others for them.' He went on, 'If you reject this, we can kill our children and women, and go out to Muhammad and his companions with drawn swords; then God will decide between us and Muhammad. If we perish, we shall perish without leaving orphans who might suffer evil, but if we are victorious, I swear we shall take their wives and their children!' They rejoined, 'Should we kill these poor creatures? What would life be to us without them?' He said, 'If you reject this, too, then consider. This is the Sabbath night, and it is possible that Muhammad thinks he is secure. Let us therefore make a sortie, and we may surprise him and his men.' But they answered, 'Shall we desecrate the Sabbath, and do on the Sabbath what none has done before save those who were afterwards transformed into apes?' Kab said at last, 'Not a man of you has, from the time his mother gave him birth, been able to hold firm to a decision for even one single night!'

Then the Qurayza asked the apostle to send them Abu Lubaba – one of the Aus, to which tribe they had been allied – that they might consult with him. When he arrived the men rose,

and the women and children crowded around him in tears, so
that he was deeply touched. They said, 'Think you that we ought
to leave the fort as Muhammad commands?' and although he said
'Yes', he drew his hand across his throat, to show that they
would be slaughtered.

Abu Lubaba said afterwards, 'By Allah! I had scarcely left
them before I realized that I had betrayed Allah and His apostle!'
When Abu Lubaba departed he did not go to the apostle of Allah,
but tied himself to one of the pillars of the mosque, saying, 'I
shall not stir from this place until Allah pardons me for what I
have done', and he swore by Allah that he would never tread
the soil of the Banu Qurayza nor be seen again in the country
where he had acted treacherously towards Allah and His apostle.
When the apostle of Allah heard of this, he said, 'Had he come to
me, I would have interceded for him; but as he has acted in this
way, I will not deliver him until Allah pardons him. Abu
Lubaba remained tied six days; whenever the hour for prayers
arrived, his wife came and untied him that he might make his
devotions. Afterwards she again bound him to the post.

In the morning the Qurayza came down from their fort to
surrender to the apostle of Allah, and the Aus begged that – as
the apostle had dealt leniently with allies of the Khazraj – he
would do the same for the allies of the Aus. The apostle said,
'Would you like one of your own people to decide their fate?'
and they welcomed it. He continued, 'Then let Sad b. Muadh
decide.' Sad had been struck by an arrow in the defence of the
Ditch, so his people mounted him on a donkey – with a leather
pillow under him, for he was a stout and handsome man – and
brought him to the apostle. They told him, 'Deal kindly with
thy allies, because the apostle of Allah has appointed thee for
this purpose.' But they entreated him too much and he said,
'Sad will take good care not to incur the censure of Allah by
fearing the censure of men.' Then some of his people went away
and lamented for the men of the Banu Qurayza, before Sad even
reached them, because Sad had spoken thus.

When Sad appeared the apostle said to the Muslims, 'Arise
in honour of your chief!' Then Sad asked, 'Do you covenant with

Allah to abide by my decision?' and they said, 'We do!' The apostle of Allah also replied, 'Yes.'

And Sad pronounced the following sentence, 'I decree that the men be killed, the property be divided, and the women with their children be made captives.' The apostle of Allah said, 'Thou hast decided according to the will of Allah, above the seven firmaments.'

The apostle of Allah imprisoned the Qurayza in Medina while trenches were dug in the market-place. Then he sent for the men and had their heads struck off so that they fell in the trenches. They were brought out in groups, and among them was Kab, the chief of the tribe. In number, they amounted to six or seven hundred, although some state it to have been eight or nine hundred. All were executed. One man turned to his people and said, 'It matters not! By God's will, the children of Israel were destined for this massacre!' Then he seated himself and his head was struck off.

Aisha, the wife of the apostle, said, 'Only one of their women was killed. By Allah! She was with me, talking and laughing, while the apostle slaughtered her countrymen in the market-place; and when her name was called, I asked, "What is this for?" and she replied, "I am going to be slain!" I asked why and she answered, "For something I have done!" Then she was taken away, and her head was struck off. But I shall never cease to marvel at her good humour and laughter, although she knew that she was to die.' She was the woman who threw a millstone down from the Qurayza fort and killed a Believer.

Now the apostle distributed the property of the Banu Qurayza, as well as their women and children, to the Muslims, reserving one-fifth for himself. Every horseman received three shares, one for himself and two for his steed, and every foot soldier one share. There were thirty-six horses present on the day of the Qurayza. The apostle dispatched an emissary to Najd with the prisoners, to barter them as slaves in exchange for horses and camels.

The apostle of Allah selected one of the Jewish women, Rayhana, for himself, and she remained with him as his slave until she died. He had suggested marriage to her, that she should wear the veil (to separate her from all other persons, as his wives did), but she replied, 'Rather allow me to remain thy slave; it will be more easy for me, and for thee.' At the time of her capture she was an enemy of Islam, and desired to remain a Jewess; so the apostle was sad and stayed aloof from her. Then one day, while he was sitting with his companions, he heard the sound of sandals behind him, and said, 'This is one who comes to inform me that Rayhana has made profession of Islam.' It was indeed so, which pleased him greatly.

After the Qurayza had been slain, and their possessions dispersed, the wound of Sad opened again and he died a martyr. In the middle of the night Gabriel, wearing a turban of gold brocade, came to the apostle, and asked, 'Who is this dead man for whom the gates of heaven stand ajar and for whom the throne quivers with joy?' At this, the apostle rose in haste and went to Sad, but he found him dead.

Sad was a corpulent man, but when the people carried him to be buried they found him light. And some said, 'Though he is stout, we never bore a lighter corpse than his.' When this came to the hearing of the apostle of Allah, he explained, 'Sad had other bearers besides you, and I swear by Him who holds my life in His hands that the angels bore the soul of Sad, and the heavenly throne shook for him.'

The apostle's victory of the Ditch was a vindication of Uhud. At Medina he was now supreme, opposed only by a minority of Hypocrites. Two of the three Jewish tribes had been exiled and the third virtually exterminated in a manner which effectively discouraged any active challenge to his position. Every dispute was now referred to him and his word was law.

It was now nearing the end of the sixth year of the Hijra and the apostle decided to set out on a pilgrimage to Mecca. This was not a warlike expedition, and it was a month not lawful for war. The apostle invited the surrounding Arab tribes and the nomad Bedouin to accompany him, for he feared the Quraysh might either attack him or prevent him from entering the Kaba. Many

Arabs delayed in joining him, so the apostle went forth with men of the Helpers, the Emigrants, and such Arabs as had appeared. He took animals suitable for sacrifice, and assumed the pilgrim garb, so that people might know he had no warlike intentions and went forth only to visit and honour the Kaba. 'He took seventy camels for sacrifice and, as the number of his men amounted to seven hundred, each camel had ten men assigned to it,' one witness recorded, but another said there were fourteen hundred men.

When the apostle reached Usfan he was told, 'The Quraysh have heard about thy expedition; and they have brought their milk-camels, and dressed themselves in leopard skins, and encamped at Dhu Tuwa, swearing to Allah they will not allow thee to enter Mecca. Khalid has, with the cavalry, already occupied Kuraul-Ghamim.' The apostle said, 'Woe betide the Quraysh! War has ruined them! How would it have harmed them to allow me to go my own way and the way of Allah? But I shall not cease to fight for the word of Allah until it becomes victorious, or until my throat is cut.' Then he said, 'Who will take us by a road which will by-pass them?' and a man of Aslam took them through a pass which was uneven and stony, until they reached an easier track.

When the Quraysh cavalry saw that the Muslims travelled by another road they hastened back to rejoin their people. When the Muslims reached the pass of al-Murar the apostle's camel knelt down, and the people said, 'She is obstinate.' He replied, 'She is not obstinate; it is not her nature to be so. But He who kept the elephant from Mecca holds this camel back, too. If the Quraysh ask this day for anything by which I may show them my kinship, I shall give it to them.' Then he said to the people, 'Camp!' and they demurred, saying, 'In this valley there is no water.' So the apostle pulled out an arrow from his quiver and gave it to one of his companions, who went down into a dried-up waterhole and pierced its bed with the arrow; then so much water gushed out that all the people drank, and they encamped around.

After the apostle had settled himself comfortably, he was visited by Budayl and several men of the Khuzaa, who talked with him and asked him the purpose of his expedition. He replied that he had come not to wage war but to visit the sacred Kaba as a pilgrim. Accordingly, they returned to the Quraysh and said, 'You are hasty in your assumptions. Muhammad has not come to fight, but to visit the Kaba.' The Quraysh persisted in their suspicions, saying, 'Although he may not have come to fight, he shall not enter against our will, nor shall the Arabs ever be able to accuse us of that.' Nevertheless, they sent observers to watch the apostle, and one of them was a devout Bedouin of the nomad tribes. When the apostle saw him approach he said, 'This man is one of the pious. Let loose the sacrificial animals before him, that he may see them!' When the man saw the animals advancing towards him from the side of the valley, wearing ornamental garlands and browsing among the salt-shrubs of this barren soil, he returned struck with awe to the Quraysh without even meeting the apostle of Allah and made his report. But they replied, 'Sit down! Thou art an Arab of the desert and have no knowledge.' Then the Bedouin became angry and said, 'My tribes did not enter into an alliance with you for such a purpose as this! Shall men be kept away from the house of Allah who have come but to honour it? You must either allow Muhammad to carry out his purpose or I and my tribes will all depart.' They replied, 'Control yourself, and we will obtain favourable terms for ourselves.'

Next they sent Urwa, another of their allies, to the apostle, and they swore they would accept his report of the matter. The apostle of Allah spoke to him as before, and told him he had not come to fight. While he was with the apostle, Urwa paid close attention to the behaviour of the companions; the apostle did not perform his ablutions without their hastening to preserve the water, nor spit without their running to gather up the saliva, and no hair fell from his head but they snatched it up. When Urwa returned to the Quraysh he said, 'I have seen the sovereign of Persia in his own country, and the sovereign of Byzantium in his own country, and the sovereign of Abyssinia in his own country; and I have not seen the king of any nation honoured as Muhammad is among his companions! I have seen a people who will never abandon him at any price! Do therefore as you think fit.'

The apostle of Allah called Uthman and dispatched him to Abu

Sufyan and the Quraysh nobles, to inform them that he had not come to fight but to make a pilgrimage to the Kaba and honour its sanctuary. Uthman reached the presence of Abu Sufyan and delivered the apostle's message, and when he had done this they said to him, 'If you yourself wish to walk around the Kaba you are at liberty to do so.' But he replied, 'I shall not do it until the apostle of Allah has done it', so the Quraysh kept him prisoner and it was reported to the apostle and the Muslims that Uthman had been murdered.

The apostle then swore, 'We shall not leave until we have fought these people,' and he called on his followers to swear an oath. This they did, in the shade of a tree, offering allegiance to the apostle and vowing not to flee from the battle. Only one man, al-Jadd, evaded taking the oath.

Soon, however, news came that the report of Uthman's death had been untrue. The Quraysh dispatched Suhayl to the apostle with these instructions: 'Make peace with him on condition that he goes away now; we cannot let the Arabs say he entered Mecca against our wish.' When the apostle observed Suhayl approaching he said, 'The Quraysh want to make peace, since they have sent that man.'

When Suhayl reached the apostle they spoke long, and at last a treaty of peace was concluded between them. When all had been arranged, only the document remained to be written. The apostle summoned Ali and said, 'Write.'

He said, 'Write "In the name of Allah, the merciful, the compassionate . . . " ', but Suhayl intervened, saying, 'I cannot accept that. Write "In thy name, o Allah." ' The apostle turned to Ali, and said, 'Write "In thy name, o Allah. This is a treaty of peace between Muhammad the apostle of Allah and . . ." ' But Suhayl intervened again. 'If I acknowledge thee to be the apostle of Allah, then I should not have fought thee! Write thy own and thy father's name.' So the apostle of Allah said, 'Write "This is a treaty of peace between Muhammad b. Abdullah and Suhayl b. Amr. They have agreed not to wage war against each other for ten years, and that their people shall not wage war against each other for ten years. If Quraysh fugitives come to

Muhammad, he will send them back; but if fugitives come to the Quraysh from Muhammad, the Quraysh will not give them up. Enmity is to end and neither deceit nor theft will be permitted between them. Any man is at liberty to make a treaty of alliance, either with Muhammad or with the Quraysh." '

It was agreed that the Muslims should give up their attempt to enter Mecca this year, but that they should have three days' clear and sole access the following year, so long as they were armed no more heavily than ordinary travellers.

When the companions of the apostle had marched out from Medina they had had no doubt that they would enter Mecca, because the apostle had had a vision; but when they witnessed the signing of this treaty and what the apostle had been obliged to submit to they were much distressed.

Now the apostle of Allah became anxious to fulfil his pilgrimage in some measure, so, after he had concluded the treaty of peace, he slaughtered the sacrifices, and had his own head shaved. When the people saw this they did the same. They were very close to the borders of the sacred territory.

The apostle began his return march, and during it the Sura *The Victory* was revealed to him. 'We have granted thee a manifest victory, that Allah may forgive thee thy past and future sins, and complete His favours to thee, and guide thee in the right way. . . . They who swear homage unto His apostle, swear homage unto Allah; the hand of Allah is over theirs. Whoever violates his oath, harms only his own soul; but whoever performs that which he hath covenanted with Allah, He will give him a great reward.' Then the Sura refers to the Arabs who lagged behind when the apostle called them to join him at the beginning of the pilgrimage. 'The Arabs of the desert who were left behind will say "Our possessions and our families held us back" ', but this is false, for they rejoiced at the possibility that you might never return. When you set forth in search of plunder, they will offer to go with you; you must refuse. Tell them they will be called to fight against a great nation, and if they obey they will be blessed, but if they turn their backs, Allah will bring on them a great chastisement. 'Allah was well pleased with the true

Believers, when they swore faithfulness to His apostle under the
tree; He knew what was in their hearts, and therefore He sent
down tranquillity of mind, and rewarded them with a speedy
victory, and they will take many spoils; for Allah is mighty and
wise. . . . He kept the hands of your enemy off from you, and
your hands from them, in the valley of Mecca, although He
could have given you victory over them . . . Otherwise you
might have struck down Believers [among the Meccans] whom
ye knew not, and thus incurred guilt unknowingly. . . . Allah
has fulfilled the vision of His apostle: You shall enter the sacred
mosque (if Allah wills it) in security, with heads shaved or
cropped, without fear. He knows what you do not.'

Before this, there had been no greater victory in Islam. War
had been rife wherever the people met, but after the treaty it
was stopped and the people felt safe and could meet and enter
into discussion and disputation; thus no intelligent man to
whom Islam was proposed in discussion failed to profess it. In
these next two years as many people adopted Islam as had done
since its first beginnings. Perhaps more. Two years later, instead
of the fourteen hundred men who went on the pilgrimage, the
apostle was able to march out with ten thousand men.

When the apostle of Allah was back in Medina a fugitive from
Mecca arrived whose name was Abu Basir. The Quraysh sent
a letter with two messengers asking for his return under the
terms of the treaty, and the apostle said to Abu Basir, 'Thou
knowest our treaty, and our religion forbids treachery! Allah
will grant deliverance and a happy outcome to thee and to those
who are likewise helpless. Return therefore to thy people.' Abu
Basir pleaded, 'Canst thou force me back to the infidels to be
seduced from my religion?' but the apostle repeated, 'Depart!
Allah will grant deliverance.'

Accordingly, Abu Basir went away with the messengers and
when they had gone as far as Dhul-Hulayfa he sat down on a
wall with them. 'Is your sword sharp?' he asked one of them.
'May I look at it?' Then Abu Basir drew it out from the man's
scabbard and killed him. The other messenger fled back to the
apostle of Allah, who was sitting in the mosque and greeted him

with 'Woe betide thee, what is the matter?' He replied, 'Thy companion has killed my companion.' Shortly afterwards Abu Basir arrived with the sword girded on and said to the apostle, 'Thou hast kept thy promise and Allah has absolved thee! Thou hast duly surrendered me into the hands of the Quraysh, but I have protected my religion.' The apostle of Allah exclaimed, 'Here is a man who would kindle a war if he had men enough!'

Abu Basir went away and halted at al-Is on the sea-coast, which was the route the Quraysh took with their caravans to Syria; and when the Believers in Mecca were told the words of the apostle, 'He would kindle a war if he had men enough', they went out to Abu Basir, as many as seventy men. Then they harassed the Quraysh, and slew every man of them that they could lay hands upon, and waylaid every caravan that passed near them, so that the Quraysh at last wrote to the apostle and begged him to allow the raiders to live in Medina as they desired, so that they would cease to harry the Quraysh, who no longer wished to have them returned to Mecca. Thus the raiders were accepted in Medina.

After this, Muhammad conceived the idea of summoning the rulers of surrounding states to listen to his teaching. The Byzantine empire appeared to be crumbling, the Christian Church was divided, and the possibilities seemed worth exploring. He determined to send out official embassies. At the same time he began to subdue or make alliances with the surrounding tribes of the peninsula.

In the seventh year of the Hijra the apostle rode out with sixteen hundred followers on an expedition against the Jewish tribe of Khaybar, about one hundred miles distant. They travelled by a route which would prevent the Khaybar from receiving assistance from their allies, the Ghatafan.

When the apostle reached the valley of Khaybar he halted his companions and prayed to Allah. 'Lord of the heavens and the earth they embrace, Lord of both worlds and all they contain, Lord of the devils and those they pervert, Lord of the winds and all that they scatter! We ask Thee for the good of this village, the good of its inhabitants, and the good of whatever is in it, and we flee to Thee for refuge from its evil, from the evil of its inhabitants, and from the evil of whatever is in it. Onward, in the name of Allah!' These words he uttered in every village he entered.

The apostle of Allah would not attack the Khaybar until next morning; if he heard the call to prayers, he would not attack, but if he failed to hear them, he would attack. 'We halted at Khaybar for the night, and the apostle waited and heard no morning call to prayer, so he mounted his horse and we mounted ours. I [the prophet's servant, Anas] rode behind Abu Talha, so close that my foot touched that of the apostle of Allah. We met a few labourers going forth early to their work, bearing spades and baskets, and when they beheld the apostle with his army they cried out and fled. The apostle said "Allah Akbar! Khaybar will be destroyed." '

The apostle occupied the Jewish forts one after the other, taking prisoners as he went. Among these were Safiya, the wife of Kinana, the Khaybar chief, and two female cousins; the apostle chose Safiya for himself. The other prisoners were distributed among the Muslims.

Bilal brought Safiya to the apostle, and they passed the bodies of several Jews on the way. Safiya's female companions lamented and strewed dust on their heads. When the apostle of Allah observed this scene, he said, 'Remove these she-devils from me!' But he ordered Safiya to remain, and threw his *reda* [cloak] over her. So the Muslims knew he had reserved her for his own. The apostle reprimanded Bilal, saying, 'Hast thou lost all feelings of mercy, to make women pass by the corpses of their husbands?'

The Muslims were in the habit of eating the flesh of their own donkeys, but on this day the apostle made various prohibitions for the future; no Believer was to eat the flesh of tame donkeys. Although the apostle of Allah forbade this flesh, he permitted consumption of horse flesh. He also declared, 'It is not lawful for a Believer to irrigate another man's harvest [to have intercourse with pregnant captives]; nor shall any Believer have intercourse with a captive woman until she has been purified; neither shall a Believer ride a captured animal which has not been assigned to him and return it, emaciated, to the joint stock of plunder; neither shall he wear a captured garment and return it, worn out, to the stock of plunder.'

After the apostle of Allah had conquered the Khaybar forts and possessions, he arrived near the forts of al-Watih and al-Sulalim, which were the last strongholds. These he besieged.

Then Marhab the Jew came out and uttered the challenge to single combat. The apostle said, 'Who will answer this man's challenge?' and Muhammad b. Maslama replied, 'I shall! I must avenge my brother who was slain yesterday!'

As they approached one another the two combatants were separated by an aged tree which served both of them as a shelter, and when one of them dodged behind it the other lopped off branches with his sword; and they continued this game until the tree was quite denuded of branches, and looked like a man. Then Marhab assailed the Muslim and struck at him, but he held out his shield and the sword stuck fast in it; then the Muslim killed him.

Ali performed great feats in the battle. 'When he approached the castle its people came out and he attacked them. A Jew struck him so as to make him drop his shield from his hand, but Ali took up a door near the fort and used it as a shield to protect himself, using it as such until Allah bestowed victory on him; then he threw it away. When all was over, I and seven men tried to turn this door over, but we had not the strength.'

After about ten days, the people realized the hopelessness of attempting to hold out; so they asked for peace and that their lives be spared. The apostle agreed, because he had already subdued all the other territory.

Kinana, the husband of Safiya, had been guardian of the tribe's treasures, and he was brought before the apostle, who asked where they were hidden. But Kinana refused to disclose the place. Then a Jew came who said, 'I have seen Kinana walk around a certain ruin every morning.' The apostle asked Kinana, 'Art thou prepared to die if we find thou knewest where the treasure was?' And he replied, 'Yes.' So the apostle ordered the ruin to be dug up, and some of the treasure was found. After that Kinana was asked again about the remainder, but he still refused to tell. The apostle of Allah handed him over to al-Zubayr, saying, 'Torture him until he tells what he knows', and al-Zubayr kindled a fire on his chest so that he almost expired; then the apostle gave him to Muhammad b. Maslama, who struck off his head.

When the people of Fadak, a Jewish town nearby, heard what was taking place they sent emissaries to the apostle to ask him to spare them and they would abandon to him all their property. He agreed. After he had reached an understanding with the people of Khaybar, they asked to be allowed to cultivate their own lands, and to retain one-half of the produce, saying, 'We know the estates better than thou, and how to cultivate them.' The apostle concluded peace with them on this basis, but added, 'If we should find it convenient to expel you, we shall do so.' The people of Fadak made peace with him on the same terms; the property of Khaybar was thus common to all the Muslims, but that of Fadak belonged to the apostle of Allah, because he had conquered it without the aid of cavalry or camels.

After the apostle of Allah had rested, the captive woman Zaynab brought him a roasted sheep. She had asked what portion of the sheep the apostle of Allah most enjoyed and, having been told that it was the leg, she put much poison into it, although she also poisoned the whole sheep. When she placed it before the apostle he took a bite, but did not swallow; Bishr likewise took a piece, but he did swallow. Then the apostle of Allah spat his out, saying, 'This bone informs me that it is poisoned.' He summoned the woman, who confessed what she had done, and asked, 'What made thee do this?' She replied, 'It is no secret to thee, what my people feel towards thee. I said to myself, "If he be only a king, we shall be delivered of him; but if he be a prophet, he will know of the poison and guard himself." ' The apostle released her, but Bishr died of the piece he had eaten.

During his last sickness, years later, the apostle said, 'I feel the vein of my heart bursting from the food I ate at Khaybar'; from these words, Muslims conclude that the apostle died a martyr of battle, as well as being favoured by Allah with the dignity of prophetic office.

The plunder of Khaybar, the richest part of the Hijaz, was

greater than any before. There were dates, oil, honey and barley, as well as sheep and camels and jewels.

Punishment for disobeying the prohibitions given on the day of Khaybar was swift. On the way back to Medina a slave of the apostle was struck by a chance arrow and killed. 'We said, "May he rejoice in paradise", but the apostle replied, "By no means! I swear that the cloak which he stole from the booty at Khaybar is now burning on him in hell!" A companion of the apostle who heard these words approached, and said "O, apostle of Allah! I took two thongs for my sandals", and he replied, "Then you will suffer two thongs of fire." '

The apostle of Allah returned to Medina and remained there for several months, sending out various raiding parties and expeditions. Then the month of pilgrimage came round and it was one year since the expedition of al-Hudaybiya when he had turned back from Mecca.

Then took place what is called the Pilgrimage of Retaliation, when the apostle retaliated against the Quraysh who had prevented him from entering Mecca in the sixth year of the Hijra by entering Mecca in the sacred month of the seventh year. The Muslims who had been kept out with him on the previous occasion now marched out on this pilgrimage, and when the Meccans heard of their approach some left the city.

But some of the people of Mecca stood near the assembly house to observe the apostle, and when he entered the mosque he threw his mantle over his left shoulder and, stretching forth his right arm, cried, 'May Allah have mercy on the man whom He shows this day to be strong.' Then he embraced the stone and went out and his companions followed him. He leapt to embrace the Yemeni stone and the Black Stone and ran thrice round the Kaba before slowing his pace. This leaping in the pilgrimage of valediction became a religious ordinance.

The apostle of Allah remained three days in Mecca and on the third day he was visited by men of the Quraysh who said to him, 'The time has expired! Depart from us!' Accordingly the apostle of Allah departed and returned to Medina.

In the first month of the eighth year of the Hijra the apostle sent an expedition to Muta on the borders of Syria and appointed over it Zayd, saying, 'If Zayd should be killed, Jafar is to take the command, and if Jafar be slain, then Abdullah b. Rawaha.' The men prepared, and when they were ready to march their number amounted to three thousand. While some of the companions of the apostle were taking leave of Abdullah b. Rawaha, he wept, and they asked, 'What makes thee weep?' He replied, 'There is no love of the world in me, nor do I grieve for you, but I heard the apostle of Allah recite a verse from the scripture of Allah, the most high and glorious, which talks of hell-fire thus: "Every one of you must go down to it. This is a decree of thy Lord which must be fulfilled." And I do not know how I shall escape after I have gone down into it.' Then the Muslims said, 'May Allah go with you and protect you, and bring you back to us safely.'

Then the people marched out, and the apostle accompanied them some way and then left them.

They marched till they reached Maan in Syria, where they heard that the Byzantine emperor, Heraclius, was encamped at Maab with 100,000 Greeks reinforced by another 100,000 men from Arab tribes commanded by a man named Malik. When the Muslims received this news they remained two nights in Maan in order to consider the matter. They said, 'Let us write to the apostle and tell him the numbers of our foe. He will either send us reinforcements, or give us some guidance.' Abdullah b. Rawaha tried to raise the spirits of his men by saying, 'What you now recoil from is just what you came in search of, martyrdom. We do not go to fight these people with numbers, strength, or multitudes, but with the religion of Allah! Therefore press on. Only one of two things can happen – both good – either victory or martyrdom.' The people exclaimed, 'By Allah! The son of Rawaha has spoken the truth!' and they set out again on their march until they came to the region of Balqa and saw the armies of Heraclius. Then a battle took place at a village called Muta.

The Muslims drew up in battle array; their right flank was commanded by a man named Qutba, and the left by Ubaya. The two armies met and fought. Zayd fought holding the banner of the apostle, until he fell to the lances of the enemy. After that, Jafar grasped the banner and fought with it, but the struggle became intense and he leapt down from his brown horse, hamstrung it to signify 'death or victory', and fought till he, too, was slain. He was the first man in Islam who hamstrung his horse. Jafar was only thirty-three years of age; he had his arms cut off in the battle and Allah replaced them in paradise with two wings on which he soars.

When Jafar was killed Abdullah b. Rawaha took the flag. He dismounted and a cousin brought him a marrow-bone, saying, 'Strengthen yourself with this, because you have undergone many hardships.' He took it and bit into it, but hearing a disturbance among the soldiers, he reproached himself, 'I am too much engrossed in life', and threw the bone away, snatched up his sword and rushed into the battle, where he fought till he was killed.

After that, Thabit snatched up the standard, crying, 'Muslims! Choose another commander!' They replied, 'Thyself', but he refused the honour and they elected Khalid, who kept off the foe and decided to retreat to spare the lives of his men. The enemy also withdrew and Khalid was able to march away with his army.

Qutba, however, who commanded the right flank of the Muslims, had killed Marith, the leader of the Arab troops reinforcing Heraclius.

When the returning army approached Medina the apostle of Allah and the Muslims went out to meet them. The children ran ahead, and the apostle followed on a mule. The people began throwing earth at the army, shouting, 'Runaways! You have fled from the path of Allah!' but the apostle said, 'They are not runaways, and if Allah pleaseth they will attack again.'

THE CONQUEST OF MECCA

AFTER the expedition to Muta, the apostle remained in Medina for a time.

The Banu Bakr had a feud of long standing with the Khuzaa which had been temporarily interrupted by the hostilities between the apostle and the Quraysh. When the treaty of peace was concluded between the apostle and the Quraysh one of the terms of the treaty was that tribes were free to enter into an alliance with either party. The Banu Bakr chose to ally with the Quraysh, and the Khuzaa with the apostle. But the Banu Bakr took advantage of the peace to revenge themselves upon the Khuzaa, and Naufal, their leader, went out with some of the tribe; his command was not acknowledged by all of them. He and his followers fell upon the Banu Khuzaa in the night and killed one man; Naufal was secretly aided by some of the Quraysh. They drove the Khuzaa back until they reached the sacred territory [Mecca] and the Banu Bakr were struck with fear, saying to Naufal, 'We have entered the sanctuary! Take heed! Fear God!' But he replied grandly, 'There is no god this day, O sons of Bakr! Take your revenge! By my life, you are accustomed to robbing sacred territory. Why not take vengeance there, too?' When the Khuzaa fell back into Mecca they sought protection in the house of Budayl.

The Banu Bakr and the Quraysh, by combining against the Khuzaa, who were allies of the apostle, had thus broken the agreement which existed between the Quraysh and the apostle, and Amr b. Salim of the Khuzaa went to the apostle and told him of the event.

The man entered the mosque of Medina, where the apostle was sitting in the midst of the people, and asked for aid and retaliation, and the apostle replied, 'It shall be done'. Then a cloud appeared in the firmament and he said, 'This cloud betokens victory.'

After that Budayl and several men of the Khuzaa also visited the apostle at Medina, uttering the same plea. When they had left to return to Mecca the apostle said to his people, 'I fancy we will have a visit from Abu Sufyan, desirous of reinforcing our alliance and extending our agreement.'

When Budayl was two days' journey from Mecca he met Abu Sufyan on his way to see the apostle. When Abu Sufyan met Budayl he asked, 'Where have you been?' and Budayl replied, 'I have been roaming the valleys.' Abu Sufyan said, 'Have you not been with Muhammad?' and Budayl replied, 'No.' After Budayl had left him, Abu Sufyan went to the place where Budayl's camels had been hobbled and, examining the dung, he found date-kernels in it; and he said, 'Budayl has indeed been with Muhammad in Medina.'

Then Abu Sufyan continued his journey till he arrived at Medina and went to the apostle of Allah, who would not speak to him. So he went to Abu Bakr and asked him to persuade the apostle to talk with him, but Abu Bakr refused; and it was the same with every one of the companions Abu Sufyan approached. At last Abu Sufyan went to the court of the mosque and cried aloud: 'Listen, ye people. I promise protection between men.' Then he mounted his camel and departed.

When he arrived back in Mecca the Quraysh asked, 'What is the news?' He told them what had taken place and they poured scorn on him, saying, 'Of what use will your words be?' and he replied, 'None. But what else could I do?'

Meanwhile, the apostle of Allah ordered preparations to be made. Abu Bakr went to his daughter Aisha, who was arranging some of the equipment the apostle would need in the campaign, and said, 'Has the apostle ordered you to make things ready for him?' She confirmed that he had and suggested Abu Bakr also prepare himself, but she said she did not know the purpose of the expedition. Later, the apostle informed the people that he was going to Mecca and ordered them to hasten their preparations.

When the apostle announced the expedition, however, Hatib – one of his trusted companions – wrote a warning letter to the Quraysh and gave it to Sara, a freedwoman, to carry to Mecca. She placed the letter on her head, plaited her hair over it, and departed. But Allah told His apostle of the letter and he sent Ali after her. Ali overtook the woman in al-Khulayqa and made her dismount; he examined her baggage, but found nothing. Then he said, 'I swear to thee by Allah! The apostle has been told no lie, nor have we been told a lie! Produce this letter, or we shall strip thee naked!' When she saw that he was in earnest she loosed the plaited hair, took out the letter and gave it to Ali. When it was brought to the apostle he sent for Hatib and asked why he had sent the warning to the Quraysh. Hatib replied, 'I believe in Allah and in His apostle. I have not altered, nor have I changed my belief. But I hoped to benefit my wife and son, who still live in Mecca.' Then the apostle pardoned him, because he had fought at Badr.

The apostle reached Marr al-Zahran with an army of ten thousand; the Bedouin tribes – the Sulaym and the Muzayna – each contributed a thousand men, and many of them Believers. Not an Emigrant nor a Helper remained in Medina. The Quraysh knew nothing of the apostle's approach, although Abu Sufyan and Budayl constantly sent out in search of news. But the apostle's uncle, al-Abbas, came out from Mecca and joined the apostle.

When the apostle of Allah was encamped at Marr al-Zahran

his uncle al-Abbas said to himself, ' "It will be the end of the Quraysh if the apostle enters Mecca by force without their having come to implore mercy from him." So I mounted the white mule of the apostle and rode out, thinking, "Perhaps I may meet some wood-gatherer who will tell the Meccans where the apostle is encamped, so that they may come out to him and ask for mercy before he has to take the town by force." After I had gone some way, I heard two voices and they were the voices of Abu Sufyan and Budayl. Abu Sufyan said, "I have never seen as many fires as there are this night, nor so great an army!" and Budayl replied, "These are the Khuzaa, aroused by war." But Abu Sufyan interrupted, "The Khuzaa are too mean and few for these to be their fires and troops."

'Then I appeared and greeted him and he asked, "What is afoot?" I said, "Woe betide thee, Abu Sufyan! That is the apostle of Allah with his people! All is over with the Quraysh!" He asked, "What is to be done?" and I told him, "If he conquers you, he will strike off your head. Mount behind me on this mule and I will take you to the apostle to ask for mercy." So he mounted behind me, but his companion returned to Mecca.

'I rode back and whenever I passed near a fire of the Muslims, they said, "This is the uncle of the apostle" and let me pass. Then I passed the fire of Umar and, seeing Abu Sufyan, he exclaimed, "This is the enemy of Allah! Praise be to Allah who has delivered him into our hands." Then he ran to the apostle, but I spurred the mule and overtook him, and hastened in to the apostle with Umar following. Umar cried, "Allow me to strike off the head of Abu Sufyan!" but I said "No. I have granted him protection." Then we argued the case and the apostle told me to guard Abu Sufyan and bring him to the apostle in the morning.

'At dawn we went to the apostle, who said to Abu Sufyan, "Is it not yet clear to thee that there is no other god save Allah!" He replied, "Had there been another god he should have proved himself by now and aided me!" The apostle continued, "Is it not yet clear to thee that I am the apostle of Allah?" Abu Sufyan replied, "I still have doubts in my mind as to that." Then I said to him, "Woe betide thee! Make profession of Islam and say,

'I testify that there is no God but Allah and that Muhammad is the apostle of Allah,' before he strikes off thy head!" So Abu Sufyan testified to the truth, and made profession of Islam. I said to the apostle, "Abu Sufyan is a man who likes to have something to boast of. Grant him some favour," and the apostle granted that any man entering the house of Abu Sufyan would be secure, so also would any man who locked himself in his own house, and so also would any man who entered the mosque.

'Then I took Abu Sufyan to a hollow of the mountain to watch the apostle and his army pass by. And all the auxiliary tribes passed first. At last the apostle appeared with the dark legion.' It was called 'dark', because of all the armour it wore; only the eyes of the men were visible. 'Abu Sufyan exclaimed, "None could resist men such as these! O Abbas, the power of your nephew has become great!" I replied, "It is the power of his prophecy!" Then I told him, "Hasten back to your people!" '

As soon as Abu Sufyan reached Mecca he cried aloud to the people, 'Muhammad comes and cannot be resisted; but whoever enters the house of Abu Sufyan will be safe!' They replied, 'Curses be upon you. Your house cannot shelter all!' so he told them, 'And whoever shuts himself up in his own house will be safe, and whoever enters the mosque will be safe!' Then the people dispersed to their houses and to the mosque.

When the apostle of Allah arrived at Dhu Tuwa he rose in his stirrups and humbly bowed his head to Allah as he observed the empty streets which betokened victory.

Starting from Dhu Tuwa, the apostle divided his troops, giving al-Zubayr command of the left wing, and giving the Helpers to Sad b. Ubada. But one of the Emigrants heard Sad chanting, 'This is a day of slaughter; today the sanctuary will be profaned.' So the apostle sent Ali after him with orders to take the banner from Sad and lead the Helpers himself. Khalid was appointed over the right flank, which consisted of the Arab tribes, and Abu Ubayda commanded the Emigrants, who were followed by the apostle himself. He entered the upper part of Mecca and had his tent pitched there.

Safwan b. Ummaya, Suhayl b. Amr, and Ikrima the son of Abu Jahl, however, had gathered some men together to fight at al-Khandama. They were attacked by Khalid's column of tribesmen, two of whom strayed from the main body and were slain; but twelve or thirteen of the idolaters were killed, and the others put to flight. The apostle had instructed his commanders not to fight against any man except those who attacked. There were, however, some enemies of Allah whom he ordered to be slain even if they were hidden in the curtains of the Kaba itself. One of these was Abdullah b. Sad; the apostle of Allah ordered him to be killed because, after having made a profession of Islam and assisted the apostle in writing the revelations, he had relapsed into idolatry, returned to his home, and taken refuge with his milk-brother. This brother concealed him, but at last brought him to the apostle of Allah, after Mecca had settled down peaceably. He pleaded for him, and it is recorded that the apostle of Allah remained silent for a long while; then he said, 'Yes.' After the man had departed, the apostle turned to his companions and said, 'I remained silent, expecting that one of you would rise and strike off his head.' Then a man of the Helpers asked, 'Why didst thou not give me a sign, o apostle of Allah?' and he replied, 'A prophet does not kill by a sign.'

Another ordered to be slain was a man who, after becoming a Muslim and being sent by the apostle of Allah with one of the Helpers to collect the poor-tax, had killed his freedman, who was a Muslim. Whilst on a journey he had halted at a caravanserai and had ordered his freedman to slaughter a kid and prepare a meal from it, but the freedman had fallen asleep. When his master awoke and found that nothing was prepared he fell upon him and killed him; then he relapsed into idolatry, and kept two singing-women, both of whom sang songs insulting the apostle of Allah, who ordered them to be killed with their master.

Another who had insulted two daughters of the apostle was also killed, and some who had persecuted the apostle himself were put to death. But some were given pardon. The daughter of Abu Talib, the uncle and one-time guardian of the apostle of Allah, told how "Two men of the tribe of my father-in-law

DESTRUCTION OF THE IDOLS

fled to me, then my brother came and said "By Allah, I shall kill them." I locked my house upon them and went to the apostle of Allah, who was in the upper part of Mecca. I found him washing himself from a kneading trough still containing vestiges of dough, whilst his daughter Fatima was shielding him with his robe. After he had finished he put on his garments and recited his morning prayers. Then he turned to me, saying "Welcome! What has brought thee here?" I told him about the two men and about my brother's wish to kill them, and he replied, "We protect whom thou protectest, and we grant safety to whom thou grantest safety! He shall not kill these two men." '

When peace reigned once more the apostle went to the Kaba and rode seven times round it on his camel, touching the sacred stone with a stick which he held in his hand. After this, he called Uthman b. Talha and took from him the key of the Kaba. This was opened to him, and he entered. There he found a pigeon made of aloe-wood, and he broke this idol with his own hand and threw it outside. The other idols stood fixed with lead, and the prophet made a sign with his stick in the direction of the idols, saying, 'Truth has arrived and falsehood has gone, because falsehood was perishable.' Nor did he point to the front of any idol, but it fell down on its back; nor did he point to its back, but it fell down on its face. Not one idol remained standing. The apostle remained at the door of the Kaba and the people from the mosque surrounded him.

Then the apostle said, 'There is no God but Allah alone. He has kept His promise, and aided His servant. He alone has put the confederates to flight. Every prerogative now lies with me save two – the guardianship of the Kaba, and the office of providing water for pilgrims.

'Killing, when heavy injury was all that was intended, must be made good by a fine of one hundred camels, among which there must be forty pregnant ones.

'People of the Quraysh! Allah has freed you from the arrogance of idolatry. All men are from Adam, and Adam is from earth! . . . How do you expect I shall deal with you?' They said, 'Well. Thou art our noble brother', and he replied, 'You may go free.' The apostle of Allah then entered the Kaba with Bilal, and ordered him to give the call to prayers.

On the day of the conquest a man entered Mecca who had murdered one of the allies of the Khuzaa. He was recognized and menaced by the Khuzaa. 'Then came Khirash, warding off the swords of the Khuzaa and shouting "Keep away!" We imagined his intention was that the people should leave the man alone, but when we moved away he himself attacked and speared him through the belly; and I can still see him with his entrails spilling out and his eyes becoming fixed. The man gasped, "You have done wrong, you Khuzaa", and then died.'

The apostle of Allah said, 'There has been enough slaughter.' He said further, 'Allah established Mecca as a sanctuary on the day He created the heavens and the earth; therefore it is a sanctuary till the day of the resurrection. No man who believes in Allah and in the resurrection may shed blood in it or fell a tree in it. It was not permitted to anyone who came before me, nor will it be permitted to anyone after me. It has been permitted to me only during this hour, because of the wrath of Allah towards the inhabitants of Mecca; now again it is a sanctuary as before. Let those of you who are present tell this to those who are absent. If any man says to you, "Verily the apostle of Allah has killed in Mecca", say "Allah has made it right for His Apostle but not for you." O, ye Khuzaa! Stay your hands from killing. You have committed a murder for which I shall pay the blood ransom; but if after my stay here anyone is killed, the relative of the murdered man will have the choice between the blood of the murderer or a ransom.'

Then the apostle paid the ransom due for the [blood of the] man whom the Khuzaa had slain. The amount of the ransom was one hundred camels.

The apostle sent out expeditions to the surrounding territory to invite the people to Allah, but not to kill. Khalid, however, used violence on one expedition, against the Jadhima, and killed some of them.

The apostle remained in Mecca for twenty-five days after the conquest.

When the Hawazin tribe heard about the conquest Allah had vouchsafed to the apostle, Malik b. Auf gathered them all together, as well as the Thaqif, the Nasr, and the Jusham, and a few men of the Banu Hilal.

Malik determined to march against the apostle of Allah, and he told the people to carry their goods, their wives and their children with them. When they encamped at Autas, the aged chieftain Durayd said, 'This is a good place for cavalry; it is neither too uneven nor too stony, neither too soft nor too hard; but why have we brought the women and children and animals?' Malik said, 'I wanted every man's family and property behind him, that he may fight for them.' Durayd snorted at him in disgust. 'Thou art a mere shepherd!' he said. 'Nothing will stop a fugitive in flight. If you conquer, only men with swords and lances will be of use to you, and if you are conquered, your families and property will be as shamed as you.' He added, 'The Kab and Kilab tribes have not joined us, so both bravery and alertness are wanting! If this were to be a day of glory and honour, neither the Kab nor the Kilab would be absent. O, Malik, you have gained nothing by bringing the most precious possessions of the Hawazin. Take them back to a safe place.' But Malik replied, 'I shall not do so. You are in your dotage and your mind is failing.'

Then Malik ordered his men, 'As soon as you see the enemy, break your swords from the scabbards and rush on the enemy as one man.'

When the apostle heard of the Hawazin massing and decided to march against them he was told that Safwan had a stock of arms and armour. He sent to Safwan, who was still an idolater, saying, 'Lend us thy arms, that we may attack our foes tomorrow. We want only to borrow them, and will return them to thee.' Safwan said 'There is no harm in that,' and gave one hundred coats of mail and sufficient arms for them.

Then the apostle marched out with two thousand Meccans and the ten thousand companions who had gone with him before to the conquest of Mecca. The apostle said, gazing at the greatness of this army of Allah, 'This day we shall not be overcome because our number is small!' They marched to meet the Hawazin.

'When we arrived at Hunayn, we descended into a valley; it was not yet day and the valley was very steep. The enemy had reached the defile before us and lay in ambush for us in every hollow, cranny and side-track. They were all ready, and attacked us before we even saw them. Only a few of our men had descended when they all fell upon us at once, so that our people fled and no man heeded his neighbour.'

The apostle turned aside, and shouted, 'Where do you flee to? Come to me! I am the apostle of Allah!' But it was useless and the camels jostled each other, and the men fled; some of the Emigrants and the Helpers, however, and others of the apostle's family, made a stand with him. Among them were Abu Bakr, Umar, Ali and al-Abbas.

When the Muslims fled some ill-disposed Meccans who had accompanied the expedition sneered. Abu Sufyan exclaimed, 'They will run as far as the sea!' and the brother of Safwan said, 'Sorcery will not suffice today!' But Safwan told him, 'Be silent! I would rather be commanded by a man of the Quraysh than of the Hawazin!'

Al-Abbas was with the apostle of Allah, holding the bridle of his grey mule. 'As I was at that time a strong man with a powerful voice, the apostle said to me, "Abbas! Shout and remind those who flee where their allegiance lies!" I did so, and the men answered, "We are at thy command." Then every man endeavoured to turn his camel, but could not because of the crush. So they took off their coats of mail, dismounted and fought their way to the apostle.'

When about one hundred men had gathered around him, they rallied and attacked the enemy, and made a good stand. The apostle alighted from his camel, and, seeing how hotly the people fought, said, 'Now at last the battle rages!' A man who took part in the battle told how, while the fight was raging, 'something like a striped black carpet came down from the sky, and settled between us and the enemy. When I looked about, I saw that black ants were strewn around the whole valley; I had no doubt that these were angels. The enemy at once fled.'

THE SIEGE OF AL-TAIF

Thus Allah put the idolaters to flight, and many were slain. Some idolaters who escaped went to al-Taif, and they included the leader, Malik; others went to Autas. But a young Believer named Rabia overtook the aged Durayd and took hold of the bridle of his camel, expecting Durayd to be a woman, because he was conveyed in a litter. When he discovered an old man, he said, 'I intend to kill you', and struck him with his sword. But this produced no effect. Durayd said, 'Your mother has armed you badly! Take my sword from behind my saddle, and strike me with it above the spine and beneath the skull. This is how I used to kill men. Afterwards, when you go to your mother, tell her you have killed Durayd; for during many a day I gave protection to the women of your family.'

On that day the apostle happened to pass near a woman around whom the people had assembled. He asked, 'What is this?' and they replied, 'A woman whom Khalid has killed.' Then the apostle said to one of the people, 'Go to Khalid and say, "The apostle of Allah forbids thee to kill child, woman or slave." '

The apostle sent an expedition after the fugitives who had gone to Autas and himself marched off to besiege the other fugitives at al-Taif. The siege was notable for the showers of arrows and red-hot metal sent down by the defenders; and, after twenty days, the apostle and his army withdrew.

They marched to al-Jirana and camped there. A deputation came from the Hawazin to discuss the six thousand children and women captives whom the apostle held, and the camels and sheep beyond number. The men of the deputation professed Islam, then said, 'We are of the same root and race as thou! Be gracious to us, and Allah will be gracious to thee!' Then a man of the Banu Sad clan of Hawazin rose and said, 'You were fostered among the Banu Sad and the nurses who suckled you are now your captives. Be kind and merciful to us; you are the best of all who have been nursed.' The apostle asked, 'Do you love your children and women more than your property?' and they said, 'Is there a choice? Restore to us our wives and children, for we love them more than our property.' He said, 'As far as my portion and that of my family is concerned, it shall be returned to you. When I have ended my noon prayers with the people, arise and say "We ask for the intercession of the apostle with the Muslims, and the intercession of the Muslims with the apostle on behalf of our children and women!" Then I shall grant your request, and intercede for you.'

When the apostle had prayed at noon the Hawazin rose and spoke as they had been instructed: the apostle replied, 'My share, and that of my family, will be given to you.' Then the Emigrants and Helpers gave theirs, but the allied tribes hesitated until the apostle said, 'Whoever still insists on his right to the prisoners, shall (if he now yields the right) receive for every captive six camels taken from the next booty Allah permits us to win.' Then the women and children were restored to the Hawazin.

The apostle asked the deputation from the Hawazin what had become of Malik and they replied, 'He is in al-Taif.' The apostle said, 'Tell him that if he comes to me as a Muslim I shall restore his family and his property to him and shall present him with a hundred camels.' Malik accepted this offer and made profession of Islam; he became a valuable Believer, and the apostle appointed him to lead three tribes who had embraced Islam. With them, he harried the idolaters.

When the apostle returned the prisoners taken at Hunayn he rode away, but his followers clamoured after him, saying, 'Distribute our shares of the camels and sheep!' At last they crowded up to him against a tree, so that his mantle was torn from his body. Then he exclaimed, 'Shame! Restore my cloak to me! By Allah, if you had captured as many beasts as there are trees in Tihama, I would distribute them to you! You have never found me to be grasping, cowardly or false!' And he turned to a camel, and pulled one hair from its haunch; he took it between his fingers, lifted it up, and said, 'I have not retained as much as this hair, beyond my one-fifth. You must give back even the most worthless articles, because theft will bring shame, fire and disgrace on the day of the resurrection for the man who steals.' Then a Helper produced a bundle of camel hair, saying, 'I took this bundle to make a cushion for the wounded back of my camel.' The apostle replied, 'I make you a present of my share in it!' The man, however, exclaimed, 'If it has come to that, I have no need of it!' and he threw the whole bundle away.

The apostle made gifts to those whose hearts he desired to win, nobles whom he wished to please. To Abu Sufyan he gave one hundred camels, and to Malik, and to Safwan and others. To some, he gave fewer than one hundred. To one man he gave only male camels, and the man was displeased instead of grateful, so the apostle said, 'Take him away, and silence him.' So they gave him camels till he was satisfied. This is what the apostle meant by 'silence him'.

One of the companions complained that a man named Juayl had received no gift, and the apostle of Allah replied, 'I swear by Him in whose hand my life is that Juayl is better than men such as those to whom I have given gifts. The gifts were given to make these men become good Muslims; but in Juayl's belief I have perfect trust.'

When the apostle had distributed his gifts to the Quraysh and to the Arab tribes he had still not given anything to the Helpers. They felt themselves aggrieved, and one man even said, 'The apostle of Allah has reverted to his own tribe.' So the apostle summoned the Helpers to him and said, 'What is this I hear about you? What has taken possession of your minds? Did I not come to you when you strayed, and Allah showed you the right direction? Were you not poor, and Allah enriched you? Were you not enemies and Allah united you?' They replied, 'Yes. Allah and His apostle were merciful to us.' He continued, 'That is no answer.'

They said, 'What shall we answer to thee? To Allah and to His apostle belong kindness and mercy.' He said again, 'If you choose, you may truthfully say, "Thou hast come to us discredited, but we believed thee. Helpless, but we helped thee! An outcast, but we sheltered thee! Destitute and we provided for thee!" Are you grieved in your souls because I have used the trifles of this world to gain the hearts of people that may become good Muslims, whereas I have had faith in the strength of your belief? Is it not enough for you to return home with the apostle of Allah, or must you have sheep and camels, too? Had it not been for the arrival of the Emigrants, I swear that I would have become as a man of Medina. Allah have mercy on the Helpers, on their sons, and on the sons of their sons.' Then the people began to weep and said, 'We are satisfied with our share and our portion.'

Afterwards the apostle went on the lesser pilgrimage and then returned to Medina.

The conquest of Mecca and of the Hawazin began a new era in Islam, and the apostle – now guardian of the holy city – had every claim to paramount power in Arabia. Religious domination was reinforced with social organization, by taxes and tributes levied from unbelievers as well as from the Faithful. Tribes came from as far away as the Yemen, the borders of Syria and Persia, to submit themselves to Muhammad. These submissions, coupled with a succession of punitive expeditions, aroused some unease in the Byzantine empire, and Heraclius was rumoured to have commanded his own feudatory border tribes to assemble to meet the challenge of the apostle.

The apostle of Allah remained in Medina for some months and then issued orders to the people to prepare for a campaign against the Byzantine empire. It happened, however, to be a time of drought and of great heat, and food was short; as the fruit crops were just ripening, the people were reluctant to obey the call. Normally, the apostle would conceal the preparations for an expedition and pretend that he was going in another direction to the one he really had in view. In the case of Tabuk, however, he made an exception because of the great distance, the difficulty of provisioning an army, and the size of the enemy force.

Many Hypocrites said to each other, 'Do not march out in the heat', because they were averse to fighting in heat, doubted the truth of Islam, and wanted to sow discontent with the prophet of Allah. Then Allah revealed this verse. 'They said, "Do not march out in the heat." Say, "The fire of hell will be hotter." Let them therefore laugh a little now, for they will weep much hereafter.'

The apostle of Allah specially exhorted the rich to furnish

money and beasts of burden and they did so, hoping for the eternal reward; Uthman was the most liberal of them, and the apostle said, 'Allah! Be pleased with Uthman; for I am pleased with him!'

Then seven Muslims came weeping to the apostle because they were poor men and could not afford beasts to carry them on the expedition. The apostle could not help them and they went away with tears pouring down their cheeks because they could not provision themselves. But Ibn Yamin met two of the Weepers and, hearing their tale of woe, presented them with a camel which they mounted, and with some dates; so they went forth with the apostle of Allah.

Meanwhile, several of the nomadic tribes asked to be exempted from the expedition, offering excuses. But Allah did not accept their words as true. Some good and true Muslims also hesitated and then remained behind when the apostle and his army left Medina. The apostle had ordered Ali to remain behind and take care of his family; but the Hypocrites reviled him, saying, 'He has been left behind because the campaign would be too much for him!' When Ali heard this he snatched up his arms and hastened after the apostle. He caught up with him at al-Jurf, but the apostle sent him back and continued his march.

In Medina, Abu Khaythama returned home one hot day and found his two wives in the arbours of his garden. Each had sprinkled her arbour with water to cool it for him, and had pre-pared a repast. He entered, and then stopped short, looking at his two wives and at the preparations they had made for him. Then he exclaimed, 'The apostle of Allah is in the sun, the wind, and the heat, while Abu Khaythama is in cool shade with a meal prepared and a fine woman, safe at home. This is not just! By Allah, I shall not enter the tent of either of you, but join the apostle. Prepare provisions for me!' They obeyed, and he went in pursuit of the apostle; as he came up with him, the people said, 'Here is a rider following along the road.' The apostle replied, 'Would that it were Abu Khaythama'; and it was.

At al-Hijr the people had no water, and complained to the apostle; then Allah sent a cloud and it rained, so that the people slaked their thirst, and gathered as much water as they needed.

Farther on during the journey the apostle's camel went astray and his companions went in search of it. A Hypocrite complained, 'Muhammad alleges that he is a prophet, and gives you news from heaven, but he knows not where his camel is!' Then the apostle said, 'I know nothing except what Allah tells me, and He has directed me to the camel; she is in the hollow in that valley, entangled with her bridle in a tree. Go and bring it.' Accordingly they went and brought the camel.

The apostle of Allah continued his march and some men began to lag behind. Each time, the apostle said, 'Leave him! If there be any good in him, Allah will help him catch us up again; but if not, Allah has delivered us of him.'

When the apostle arrived in Tabuk, he was visited by John, the Christian governor of Ayla, who made peace with the apostle and paid him tax. Then the Jewish inhabitants of Jarba and Adhruh also came and paid him tax; and the apostle gave them a document, and one to John in the following terms. 'In the name of Allah, the merciful, the compassionate! This is a guarantee from Allah and from Muhammad, the prophet and apostle of Allah, to John and to the inhabitants of Ayla! Their ships and their caravans on sea and on land are under the protection of Allah and Muhammad His prophet, as are those people of Syria, of Yemen, and of the sea-coast who escort them. Whosoever commits a crime against them will be unable to atone for it with property; but his life will be at the mercy of all. The people of Ayla shall not be kept back from water nor hindered from taking any direction in which they choose to proceed, whether by land or by sea.'

Next the apostle of Allah dispatched Khalid to the Christian, Ukaydir, at Duma. It was a clear moonlit night and the cavalry, led by Khalid, took Ukaydir wholly by surprise and brought him to the apostle of Allah, who spared his life and granted him peace on condition that he paid tax. Then he set him free and he returned to Duma. The apostle remained about ten days at Tabuk, and then returned to Medina. [There was no sign of Heraclius or the rumoured invading force.]

THE PENANCE OF KAB

Before the apostle had left for Tabuk he had been approached by some men who said, 'We have built a mosque for the sick and the needy, for wet and for cold nights, and we are anxious that thou shouldst come and pray therein.' He had replied, 'I am on the verge of leaving, but when we return, we shall, if Allah willeth, pay you a visit and pray in the mosque.' When he alighted at Dhu-Awan, an hour's ride from Medina, on his return, information was sent down to him from Allah about the mosque. He called two of his followers and said, 'Go to this mosque, whose people are unrighteous; destroy it; burn it.' So they departed in haste and took a blazing date-branch to the mosque. Although there were people in it, they burned and destroyed it. This was the verse of the Koran revealed concerning this matter: 'And those who erected a mosque out of opposition and unbelief and to cause a schism among the Believers – they will say "We desired nothing but good". Allah knows they lie. Enter no such mosque.'

The apostle of Allah was greatly displeased with those who had remained behind and evaded the expedition. He dismissed the false excuses of the Hypocrites, and dealt sternly with three staunch Believers who had remained behind through procrastination, not illwill. He prohibited the people from speaking to these three, who included the poet Kab, who had told the truth and made no excuses for himself. 'The people avoided us and changed their behaviour, so that I seemed to have become a stranger even to myself, and the country seemed to me to differ from the one I had known. We remained fifty days in this condition. My companions remained secluded and sat in their houses, but I, being the youngest and most active, used to go out and attend prayers and walk about in the public bazaars. But nobody spoke to me. I went also to the apostle and saluted him while he was sitting in his assembly after prayers; I would ask myself whether he had moved his lips to return my greeting. Then I prayed near him and kept glancing at him, and saw that he watched me while I prayed, but looked away when I turned towards him.

'After this estrangement had lasted some time, I became

impatient and climbed over the garden-wall of my cousin, whom I loved more than any other man, and saluted him. But he took no notice of me. Then I said, "Do you not know that I love Allah and His apostle?" He remained silent, and only replied after I had thrice repeated this question. "Allah and His apostle know best!" he said. Now my eyes overflowed with tears and I went to the bazaar and walked about. A Nabati trader from Syria came to me and handed me a letter from the king of Ghassan. It was wrapped in a silken envelope, and said, "We hear your master has slighted you; come instead and be welcomed by us." Then I said to myself, "Here is a further ordeal, that an idolater should hanker for my company!" And I burned the letter.

'We remained thus for forty days, when a messenger came to me and said, "The apostle orders you to separate from your wife!" I asked, "Am I to divorce her?" but he said, "No! Only separate from her, and do not approach her!" So I told my wife to go to her family until Allah decided the matter according to His pleasure.

'In this condition we remained for ten days more, so that fifty days had elapsed from the time the apostle of Allah forbade the people to speak to us. On the morning of the fiftieth day I made my prayers at the top of the house as Allah decreed, and life was a burden to me. I had pitched a tent on the hill near Medina and I was there when I heard a man shouting, "Here are glad tidings!" Then I prostrated myself, because I knew that deliverance was at hand. When the apostle had dismissed the people after morning prayers he announced that Allah had pardoned us, so they ran to tell us. Some ran to my two companions; one man came to me on horseback, but another hastened up the mountain, and his voice reached me faster than the horse. When he arrived with the good news I took off my garments and gave them to him in gratitude. But by Allah! I had no others there that day and was compelled to borrow garments to cover myself!

'I went to pay my respects to the apostle and was met by many who congratulated me on the pardon, saying, "May the forgiveness of Allah bring you fortune!" At last I reached the mosque, where the apostle was sitting among the people. Talha rose, saluted me, and congratulated me; but no other Emigrant did so. (I never forgot this kindly act of Talha.) When I saluted the apostle his face was lit up with joy, and he said, "Rejoice at thy happiest day since thou wast begotten!" I asked, "Is the forgiveness from thee or from Allah?" and he replied, "It is from Allah!" Whenever the apostle gave good news his face would glow like the moon. I sat in front of him and said, "One sign of my penitence shall be that I shall divest myself of all my goods for the sake of Allah and His prophet!" but the apostle replied, "Keep some of thy property for thyself; it will be better for thee." I said, "Then I shall retain only the share I received in Khaybar. Allah has forgiven me because I invented no excuses; therefore another sign of my penitence will be that I shall never speak anything but the truth as long as I live." Since I uttered those words to the apostle I know of no man whom Allah can have found more truthful than myself. From that day to this I have uttered no untruth, and I pray that Allah will always find me so.'

The apostle returned from Tabuk in the month of Ramadan. In the same month he received a deputation from the Hawazin who had been besieged in the fortress of al-Taif. After their discussion, they parted, and the apostle was followed by one of the deputation, a leader named Urwa, who then made profession of Islam. He asked that he be permitted to return to his tribe, who remained idolaters, but the apostle replied, 'They will kill thee!' Urwa said, 'I am dearer to them than their firstborn sons', and indeed he was much beloved by them. So he went back to al-Taif to invite his people to Islam, hoping they would not resist him, but when he made his appearance in the upper part of one of his houses and invited them to Islam, they shot arrows at him from every direction and one struck and killed him. Thus he became a martyr.

After this, the people at al-Taif deliberated several months, and arrived at the conclusion that they were not strong enough to fight all the Arabs around them who had paid homage to

Muhammad and made profession of Islam. Then they determined to send another deputation to the apostle of Allah and proposed that Abdu Yalil should go; but he refused, because he feared that when he returned he might be treated as Urwa had been. As he refused to go alone, they decided to send with him six men representing the several tribes.

When the emissaries came to the apostle he had a tent pitched for them near his mosque, and Khalid acted as intermediary until agreement was concluded. They would not eat of any food sent them by the apostle unless Khalid had tasted it first, until the time when they professed Islam and settled their treaty. One of the emissaries' stipulations was that the apostle should permit them to keep their goddess al-Lat for three years; but he refused. Then they insisted upon one year, but he again refused. Then they pleaded for a single month, but he refused. They said that they merely wished to spare the feelings of the weaklings, the women and the children among them, and that they were nervous of frightening their people by destroying the goddess before Islam was fully established in al-Taif. But the apostle still refused, and insisted on sending Abu Sufyan and al-Mughira back with them to destroy her.

The Hawazin further asked to be excused from prayers and from destroying their idols with their own hands. The apostle replied, 'We shall excuse you from breaking your idols with your own hands. But as for prayers! What is there good in a religion which has no prayers!' They said, 'We shall comply even though it be a humiliation!'

When they had made their profession of Islam the apostle appointed over them Uthman b. Abul-As, the youngest of them in years, but the most diligent in learning the religious doctrines of Islam. He said to Uthman, 'Be brief in prayers, and estimate the people according to the weakest of them; among them thou wilt find old ones, and young ones, weak ones and needy ones.'

The document which the apostle gave to the deputation permitted certain privileges to the inhabitants of al-Taif. 'In the name of Allah, the merciful, the compassionate. From Muhammad the prophet, who is the apostle of Allah, to the Believers!

The forests of Wajj and the game therein shall not be injured, and any man found disobeying this shall be scourged and stripped of his garments. Any who transgress this command must be brought to the prophet, Muhammad, for this is a matter which concerns him who is the apostle of Allah.'

The apostle spent the remainder of the month of Ramadan and the next two months in Medina, and then dispatched Abu Bakr in command of the pilgrimage in the ninth year of the Hijra. The idolaters also made their customary pilgrimage.

When Abu Bakr and the Muslims who accompanied him had departed the *Declaration of immunity* was sent down by Allah. It proclaimed that Allah and His apostle, after this pilgrimage, were absolved from observance of all treaties which they had previously made with idolaters. 'Therefore if you [the idolaters] repent, this will be better for you; but if you turn your backs, know that you cannot weaken Allah! And warn those who disbelieve that there will be grievous punishment. An exception shall be made for those idolaters who have not infringed treaties, and who have given no one aid against My prophet. Their treaties shall be observed until their terms expire, because Allah loves those who are pious.

'When four months have elapsed', the instruction to Muhammad continued, 'kill the idolaters wherever you find them; make them prisoners, surround them, and besiege them wherever they may be. But if they repent and pray according to the command of Allah and pay the tax, then set them free, because Allah is forgiving and merciful.'

When the *Declaration of immunity* was revealed to the apostle, he sent for Ali and said to him, 'Go with this account of the first part of the *Declaration of immunity*, and proclaim it among the people on the day of sacrifice when the pilgrims assemble in Mina. Say "No infidel can enter paradise, and after this year no idolater will be allowed to make the pilgrimage, or walk around the Kaba naked; he who has a treaty with the apostle of Allah may depend on it, until its appointed span!" '

Ali mounted the apostle's she-camel and pursued Abu Bakr

and went with him to Mecca. When the day of sacrifice arrived Ali rose and made his proclamation to the people as he had been commanded. Then he gave four months' grace from the day of this proclamation, so that every tribe might return home in security.

Allah said, 'Fear no idolaters; rather fear Allah. Attack them! Allah desires to punish them by your hand, to put them to shame and give you the victory over them. . . .

'The Quraysh have said, "We are the people of the sacred city, providers for the pilgrims, and builders of the Kaba; and there is none more excellent than we." But only he shall visit the mosque of Allah who believes in Allah and in the day of judgement. . . . Do you imagine that giving drink to pilgrims and visiting the holy mosque is the same as believing in Allah, and fighting for the word of Allah? . . . The idolaters are impure; let them not approach the holy mosque after this year.'

Then Allah promised to recompense the Believers for the trade they would lose through pursuing this course, and assigned to them tax and tributes levied from the Jews and Christians. He spoke of the wickedness and superstition of those who lived according to the Old and New Testaments, saying, 'Priests and monks devour the property of men, in vanity, and obstruct the way of Allah. For those who lay up gold and silver, and spend it not in furthering the word of Allah, there will be grievous chastisement.' Then he said, 'The number of months is twelve in the book of Allah since the day He created the heavens and the earth, and four of these months are sacred [war is forbidden in them]. This is the true religion. Do not therefore act unrighteously in them as the idolaters have done. . . .'

Then he spoke of the distribution of property. 'Alms are due to the poor, and the needy; to those whose hearts are to be won over; for the redemption of slaves, and the freeing of debtors; to further the word of Allah, and to give to travellers. This is an ordinance from Allah, and Allah knows all and is wise. . . .

'O, prophet! Wage war against the Unbelievers and against the Hypocrites who utter belief but have none, and be severe unto them, for their abode shall be in hell. The apostle and those who truly believe went to the holy war [the Tabuk expedition] with their wealth and their lives; they will enjoy good fortune and be happy. . . .' The first of the Emigrants and the first of the Helpers have special favour in the sight of Allah and their reward in paradise will be great.

When the apostle of Allah had conquered Mecca and completed the campaign of Tabuk, and when al-Taif had surrendered and made profession of Islam, deputations of Arabs arrived from all directions. This, the ninth year after the Hijra, was called the Year of Deputations. The Arabs had delayed professing Islam until they saw how the affair between the apostle and the Quraysh would end, because the Quraysh were the leaders of men, the people of the Kaba and of the sacred territory, and they were acknowledged as the descendants of Ishmael, son of Abraham. Not one chief of the Arabs denied this. But when Mecca was conquered and the Quraysh submitted to Islam, the Arabs knew that they themselves were not strong enough to wage war or to show enmity to the apostle of Allah. So they entered into the religion of Allah in droves, arriving from all directions.

When a deputation from the Banu Tamim arrived they entered the mosque and shouted to the apostle to come out from his private apartments. This shouting displeased the apostle, but he went out to them, and they said, 'We come to contend with you for glory! Allow our poet and orator to speak!' Then Utarid, their orator, rose and declaimed the virtue and greatness of the Banu Tamim: 'Who is like us among men? Are we not chiefs of the human race and most excellent of all?' and more to similar effect.

He sat down, and the apostle called on his own orator, Thabit, to reply to the harangue. Thabit rose and extolled the 'most noble descent, most high dignity, and most favoured reputation of the Muslims'.

Then the poet of the Banu Tamim rose in his turn to enter the contest of words, and when he had done the apostle sent for Hassan. Hassan waxed long and eloquent, and when he fell silent at last, one of the Banu Tamim exclaimed, 'This poet is

THE LIFE OF MUHAMMAD

more poetical than ours, and this orator more eloquent than ours; and their voices are clearer than ours.' So they made profession of Islam, and the apostle gave them valuable gifts.

After many such tribes had come to Islam and others had given submission to the apostle, he sent out a number of his followers to instruct people in Islam and collect the public taxes. He placed Muadh over these collectors.

When he sent Muadh out he gave him instructions and the following injunction, 'Be gentle and not harsh; announce the good tidings; give no offence. When thou arrivest among people who are of the scripture [Christians and Jews], they will ask thee, "What is the key to paradise?" Say, "The testimony that there is no God but Allah alone, and he has no associate." ' Accordingly, Muadh departed, and when he reached Yemen he acted as the apostle had ordered him.

Certain tribes still remained who had not accepted Islam, so the apostle sent Khalid to the Banu al-Harith in Najran, with orders to give them three days to embrace Islam, and thereafter to subdue them if they refused. Khalid sent out mounted parties in every direction to invite the people to Islam, shouting, 'Make profession of Islam and you will be saved!' The people responded to the call and entered the religion, and Khalid remained among them to teach them the doctrines of Islam, the Koran, and the ordinances of the apostle of Allah. After a time, Khalid brought a deputation of the Banu al-Harith to meet the apostle at Medina.

When they arrived the apostle at first asked, 'Who are these people? They look like men from India!' Then they stood before him and saluted him, and said, 'We testify that thou art apostle of Allah, and that there is no God but Allah!' Then they returned to their people and the apostle appointed Qays to be their leader, and sent Amr to instruct them in Islam and teach them the doctrine and collect alms from them. Amr was given detailed orders concerning what the al-Harith should be taught.

'He [Amr] is to prohibit any man from praying in a small garment unless it be such that both its extremities may be wrapped round the shoulders; nor may anyone perform his prayers in such a garment as will expose his private parts. He must also prohibit men from plaiting their hair and allowing it to hang down their backs. He must prohibit the people, in case of a quarrel, from calling out their tribes to help them – they should invoke the aid of Allah alone; and those who fail to call upon Allah, but call instead upon their tribes, must be visited by the sword until they call upon Allah. He is to command the people to perform religious ablution before their prayers, by washing their faces, and their hands as far as the elbows and their feet as far as the ankles; they must likewise wipe their heads as Allah has ordained. He commands that the prayers be held at their due seasons, with bowing and prostration, when the morning dawns and at noon when the sun begins to decline; the afternoon prayers are to be held when the sun declines, and the evening when the night sets in, but they are not to be delayed until the stars begin to appear; and the night devotions are to be held during the first part of the night. The presence of the people at Friday prayers, when the call goes forth, is incumbent upon them as is the ablution beforehand.'

The apostle gave many other instructions. And he commanded Amr to take one-fifth of any booty for Allah, as well as the legal alms from the land. These consisted of 'one-tenth from land irrigated by springs and rains; one-twentieth from land irrigated with buckets. For every ten camels, two sheep; for every twenty camels, four sheep; for every forty horned cattle, one cow; for every thirty, one male or female calf entering its third year; for every forty sheep, a young one old enough to graze alone. This is an ordinance from Allah ordained to Believers as the required alms; but he who is more generous will win merit. Any Jew or Christian who persists in his religion is not to be turned away from it, but must pay one golden dinar or its equivalent in cloth. He who pays this will be protected by Allah, and His prophet; he who refuses is an enemy of Allah and His prophet, as well as of all Believers. The grace of Allah be upon Muhammad; and salutation to him with the mercy and blessings of Allah.'

The apostle of Allah sent his Amirs [representatives] and officials to collect the poor-tax of all the districts subject to Islam.

A man named Musaylima, who claimed he, too, was an apostle of Allah, wrote to the apostle the following letter. 'From Musaylima, the apostle of Allah, to Muhammad the apostle of Allah! Greetings! I am thy partner in authority. One half of the earth will belong to us and the other half to the Quraysh, but the Quraysh people are sinners.' With this letter he sent two messengers, and the apostle of Allah, having read the letter, asked them, 'What do you say to this?' They replied, 'We say what he says.' The apostle exclaimed, 'If it were not that messengers are guaranteed their safety, I would strike off your heads.' Then he wrote these lines, 'In the name of Allah, the merciful, the compassionate! From Muhammad the apostle of Allah to Musaylima the liar! Salutations to him who follows the true guidance! The earth belongs to Allah, and He bestoweth it upon those of His servants whom He will. The pious will meet with a happy destiny.'

In the next year, the tenth of the Hijra [AD 630], the apostle made preparations for the pilgrimage, and ordered his people to do the same. He took with him sacrificial animals, and ordered that all the people (except those who had brought sacrificial animals) should, after visiting the holy places, divest themselves of their pilgrim habit. Then he entered Mecca, and all the people who had brought no sacrificial animals divested themselves of their pilgrim habit.

The apostle of Allah had sent Ali to Najran, and Ali returned to Mecca to rejoin the apostle during the pilgrimage. He gave him a report on the journey to Najran and the apostle then said, 'Go and walk round the Kaba; then divest thyself of the state of pilgrim as thy friends have done.' But Ali said, 'When I assumed the state of a pilgrim, I said, "I dedicate myself to Thee, Allah, as Thy apostle Muhammad has done." ' Ali had no sacrificial animals, so the apostle of Allah gave him part of his own. And the apostle of Allah slaughtered the sacrifices in both their names.

During this pilgrimage the apostle of Allah clarified sacred usages and ceremonies to the people He preached a sermon, in which he explained many things. After giving praise to Allah, he said, 'Listen to my words, because I do not know whether I shall meet you again here after this occasion. Your blood and your property shall be sacred to you until you meet your Lord. You will meet your Lord and He will examine you about your deeds. Whoever has charge of another person's wealth, let him return it to the man who has deposited it. Usury is forbidden, but capital belongs to you. Do no wrong, and none shall wrong you. Time has come full circle since the day when Allah created the heavens and the earth. The number of months with Allah amounts to twelve months, four of which are sacred.

'You have rights over your wives, and they have rights over you. Your rights over them are that they shall allow no one of whom you disapprove to enter your bed, nor must they commit open fornication; if they commit it, Allah permits you to exclude them from your beds, and to beat them (with moderation). Treat your wives well, because they cannot fend for themselves; you have taken them on trust from Allah, and they are yours by the grace of Allah.

'Ponder my words. I have left with you knowledge which, if you follow it, will preserve you for ever from going astray; the words of Allah and the injunctions of His apostle. Know that every Muslim is brother to every Muslim. No man may take anything from his brother save what is freely given.'

Thus the apostle terminated his pilgrimage. This was the pilgrimage of instruction and valediction, because after it the apostle of Allah went no more on pilgrimage. It was 'The Farewell Pilgrimage'.

When the apostle returned to Medina he dispatched envoys from among his companions to various rulers, and sent letters in which he invited them to accept Islam. He said to his companions, 'Do not resist me as his disciples resisted Jesus.' His companions asked, 'How did the disciples resist?' He said, 'He sent them as I send you; but those whom he sent to a place near by were pleased, and obeyed, whereas those whom he sent to a distance, went unwillingly and considered it a hardship. Jesus complained to Allah; and everyone who had considered it a hardship was the next morning able to speak the language of the nation to whom he had been sent.'

The apostle of Allah sent envoys to the Caesar of Rome, the king of Persia, the Negus of Abyssinia, the Byzantine emperor, the kings of Alexandria, of Uman, and of Bahrein and to many others.

While the people were thus engaged the last illness of the apostle began in which Allah took him to Himself, to His mercy and grace. The malady began thus. He had given orders for an expedition to set out to the borders of Syria; that night, his manumitted slave recorded, 'The apostle of Allah awoke me in the middle of the night and said, "I am commanded to implore pardon for the dead in the cemetery!" So I went there with him, and when he stood among the dead, he exclaimed, "Peace be upon you, tenants of these graves! May the state you are in be better than that which lies in store for mankind! Rebellions are setting in like waves of darkness. They will follow each other, and the last will be worse than the first". Then he turned to me and said, "I have been offered a choice between the treasures of this world and everlasting life, or paradise and the meeting with my Lord. I have chosen the second." I replied, "Thou art my father and my mother; take the treasures of this world now and paradise afterwards." But he continued, "No. I have chosen to meet my Lord." After that, the malady of the apostle began, and Allah took him away.'

According to Aisha, 'The apostle of Allah returned from the cemetery to me. I had a headache and complained "My head! My head!" And he replied, "No, Aisha. *My* head!" Then he said, "Wouldst thou be distressed to die before me, that I might stand over thee and enshroud thee, and pray for thee, and bury thee?" But I exclaimed, "If that were to happen, I can see thee no sooner bury me than return to my house, to celebrate thy wedding with some other woman!" The apostle smiled, and, though the malady began to develop, he continued to make the round of his wives until, in the house of Maymuna, it overcame him. Then he called his wives to ask their permission to spend in my house such time as he was ill, and permission was granted to him.'

The total number of the apostle's wives was thirteen. After Khadija and Aisha, he married Sauda; then Zaynab, who had been the wife of his freed slave, Zayd, who divorced her that she might wed the apostle; and Umm Salama, to whom he gave as dowry a mattress stuffed with palm fibres, a cup, a dish, and a handmill. Then he wed Hafsa; and Umm Habiba, as a compliment to Abyssinia; and Juwayriya from among the captives of the Banu Mustaliq; and Safiya from among the captives at Khaybar; and Maymuna, and Zaynab b. Khuzayma, who was called 'Mother of the Poor' because of her compassion and kindliness.

With these eleven wives the apostle consummated his marriages. Two died before him, namely Khadija and Zaynab, but nine survived him. With two others he did not consummate marriage: with Asma, who had the white spots of leprosy and whom he sent back to her family; and with Amra, who had lately been an Unbeliever and who fled to Allah for refuge from the apostle of Allah. He said, 'Who flees for refuge to Allah is well protected', and sent her back to her family.

At the time of his illness, Aisha said, 'The apostle of Allah came walking between two men, with his head wrapped in a cloth, and he walked slowly till he entered my house. Then the apostle fainted, and his malady became worse. He said, "Pour seven leather bags of cold water from the well over me, that I may go out to the people, and give them my last injunctions." So we seated him in a tub and poured water over him till he said, "Enough! Enough!" '

The apostle went out with his head bandaged, and sat upon the pulpit. The first words he spoke were words of prayer for those who had fallen at Uhud; for them he implored pardon and again prayed at some length. Then he said, 'Allah has given one of His servants the choice between this world and the next, and he has chosen to be with Allah.' Abu Bakr understood these words and knew that he meant himself; so he wept, saying, 'Nay. We shall give our own lives and those of our children for thine.' But the apostle said, 'Look to these doors which open into the mosque, and close them all save those which lead to the house of Abu Bakr, because I have known no better companion than he.'

While the apostle was sick the people delayed the expedition he had commanded, but he said, 'Carry out the expedition to the Syrian border', and the people hastened their preparations.

He commanded the Emigrants to treat the Helpers well, saying, 'Other groups increase, but the Helpers must remain the same in number and cannot increase. They were my asylum and gave me shelter. Be kind to those who are kind to them, and punish those who injure them.' Then the apostle entered his house, and the sickness overcame him so that he fainted.

The wives of the apostle gathered to consult, and all agreed that they ought to pour medicine into his mouth. The uncle of the apostle, al-Abbas, offered to pour it himself. When the apostle recovered from his swoon he asked, 'Who has done this to me?' and they replied, 'Thy uncle!' He said, 'This is a medicine brought by women from Abyssinia. Why have you done this?' Then his uncle replied, 'We feared thy having pleurisy', and the apostle said, 'That is a disease with which Allah the most high and glorious has not afflicted me! Let no one remain in this house without swallowing some of this medicine, except my uncle.' Accordingly even Maymuna swallowed some – although she was fasting at the time – because the apostle swore that all must taste it as a punishment for what they had done to him.

According to Aisha, 'When the apostle had become very ill, he said, "Order Abu Bakr to pray with the people!" And I replied, "Abu Bakr is a tender-hearted man with a weak voice, and he weeps much when he reads the Koran." But he said, "Order him to pray with the people!" I objected only to spare my father, because I knew the people would never wish another man to stand in the prophet's place, and would blame my father for any evil which might occur.'

On the Monday on which Allah took His apostle he went out to the people at their morning prayers. The curtain at Aisha's door was lifted, the door opened, and the apostle of Allah came out and stood in the doorway. When the Muslims caught sight

of him they were almost diverted from their prayers through joy
at his presence. He signalled them to continue their devotions,
and smiled with pleasure as he watched them pray; never had
the watchers seen him wear a more beautiful expression than then.
After the prayers he addressed the people in a voice loud enough
to be heard outside the door of the mosque. He said, 'The fire
is kindled, and confusion descends like darkness. But ye have
nothing to reproach me for. I have allowed only what the Koran
allows, and have forbidden what the Koran forbids.' When the
apostle had finished speaking Abu Bakr said, 'Apostle of Allah!
I see thou hast risen this morning, by the favour and grace of
Allah, in the state of health we love to see thee in!' Then the
people went to their homes, satisfied that the apostle was recovered from his illness.

But al-Abbas had said that morning to Ali, 'I swear by Allah
that I have seen death in the face of the apostle.' And he was not
mistaken.

Aisha said, 'When the apostle of Allah returned that morning
from the mosque he rested on my lap.' Usama, in command of
the Syrian expedition, had camped outside Medina, but when he
heard the apostle was dangerously ill he went down to Medina
with his army. 'When I went in to the apostle he had already lost
the power of speech and said nothing; but he lifted his hands to
heaven and then again lowered them, and I knew he was praying
for me.'

According to Aisha, 'a man of the family of Abu Bakr happened to enter with a fresh toothpick in his hand and the apostle
of Allah looked at it in such a way that I knew he wanted it. I
asked, "Shall I give thee this toothpick?" and he replied, "Yes".
So I took it and chewed it until it became soft and gave it to him.
He rubbed it against his teeth, more sharply than I had ever seen
him do, and then he laid it down again. Then I found that he was
becoming heavy in my lap, and I looked at him and saw that his
eyes were turned upwards; and he said, "Nay! Rather the
companion in paradise!" I had often heard the apostle say,
"Allah takes no prophet away without giving him a choice", and
when he died his last words were, "Rather the companion in

paradise". Then I thought, "He has not chosen our companion-ship". And I said to him, "The choice was thine, and I swear by Him who sent thee that thou hast chosen what is right." Then the apostle of Allah died, at noon on Monday.

'The apostle died on *my* breast, despite my foolishness and youth. I placed his head on a cushion, and then I rose and began to strike my face and beat my breast with the other women.'

Now Umar rose before the people and said, 'Some Hypocrites say that the apostle of Allah is dead! He has not died, but has departed to his Lord, just as Moses left his people for forty days, and returned to them when it was rumoured he was dead. By Allah! The apostle will return just as Moses did, and the hands and feet of the men who have said that the apostle is dead will be cut off!'

Abu Bakr arrived, and alighted at the door of the mosque while Umar was talking thus. But he took no notice, and went in to see the body of the apostle in the house of Aisha. It was laid out and shrouded with a striped mantle. This he removed from the face of the apostle and, kissing it, said, 'Thou art to me as my father and mother! Thou hast tasted the death which Allah decreed for thee; but after it, no death will ever come to thee again.' Then he covered the face of the apostle and went out. He went to Umar and said, 'Gently! Listen to me!' but Umar paid no attention, and continued his speech.

When Abu Bakr saw that he would not listen he himself turned to the people, who left Umar and came to him. Then he gave praise to Allah and said, 'Let all who adored Muhammad know that Muhammad is dead, and let all who adore Allah know that Allah is eternal and never dies.' Then he recited the verse 'Muhammad is but an apostle. Other apostles have passed away before him. If he die or be slain will ye turn back? He who turns back does no injury to Allah; and Allah will surely reward those who give thanks.' And it was as if the people had never heard this verse until Abu Bakr recited it then.

Umar told thereafter how 'When Allah had caused His apostle to die, the Helpers disagreed with the Emigrants about what should next be done, and they gathered to discuss it. I said to Abu Bakr, "Let us go to our brethren the Helpers", and we went, and sat down with them. Then their orator pronounced the Confession of Faith, uttered due praise to Allah, and said, "We are the Helpers of Allah and the army of Islam, and you Emigrants are a part of us." And they intended thus to take dominion away from us. When he ceased to speak I prepared to reply and had already thought out an oration which pleased me when Abu Bakr said, "Gently, Umar!" And I was unwilling to anger him.

'Then he spoke and he was more learned and dignified than I. There was not a sentiment I had intended to use which he did not express in the same or even in a better way than I could have done. He said, "Whatever good qualities you claim, you are possessed of! But the Arabs concede supremacy only to us of the Quraysh, who are the centre of the Arab world by heredity and position. I propose to you one of these two men as leader and you may pay homage to whichever you prefer!" Then he took hold of my hand and that of Abu Ubayda. This was the only sentiment in his speech which displeased me, for I would rather have had my head struck off than govern over a man so great as Abu Bakr.

'Then a Helper rose and said, "Let there be one Amir selected from the Helpers, and one from the Emigrants", and many voices were raised and there was confusion. So, fearing dissension, I cried to Abu Bakr to stretch out his own hand and I paid him homage. Then all paid him homage.'

Finally, Abu Bakr spoke again. He said, 'I am appointed to govern you, although I am not the best of you. If I act well you must aid me, and if I act unjustly you must correct me. Truth is faithfulness and falsehood is treachery! No nation has failed to fight for Allah but Allah has punished it with abasement; nor has wickedness become widespread without Allah sending calamity. Obey me as long as I obey Allah and His prophet! But should I rebel against Allah and His prophet you will owe me no obedience! Rise to your prayers and may Allah have mercy on you!'

On Tuesday, after allegiance had been paid to Abu Bakr, the people made preparations for the burial of the apostle of Allah. Ali, al-Abbas and his sons al-Fadl and Qutham, with Usama and Shuqran, took it upon themselves to wash the corpse. Ali leaned the body against his own breast, while al-Abbas, al-Fadl and Qutham helped to turn him. Usama and Shuqran poured the water whilst Ali washed him. Ali said, 'Thou art my father and my mother! How beautiful thou art, alive and dead.' And there was nothing distasteful, as with other dead bodies, in the corpse of the apostle of Allah.

Aisha said, 'When they were about to wash the apostle, they disagreed and said, "By Allah! We do not know whether we ought to strip the apostle of Allah as corpses are usually stripped, or whether to wash him in his clothes". As they were discussing, Allah sent sleep upon them so that there was not a man among them who did not slumber; and they heard a voice which they knew not, saying, "Wash the prophet in his garments!" They rose and washed the apostle of Allah in his shirt, pouring water over it, and rubbing it with their hands, so that the shirt was between their hands and the body.' After the washing had been completed, the apostle was wrapped in three garments.

When the body had been arranged and laid out on the couch in his own house the Muslims knew not where to bury him. One said, 'Let us bury him in his mosque.' Another said, 'Let us bury him with his companions.' And Abu Bakr said, 'I have heard the apostle of Allah say that every prophet should be buried on the spot where he died.' Accordingly the bed on which the apostle had been resting was lifted up, and the grave dug under it. But there was doubt about the form of the grave.

Abu Ubayda was accustomed to dig graves plainly, according to the fashion of Mecca, but Abu Talha, the grave-digger of Medina, dug them in a vaulted shape. Al-Abbas therefore called two men, and said to one of them, 'Go to Abu Ubayda', and to the other, 'Go to Abu Talha.' He added, 'Allah, choose for Thy apostle.' Abu Ubayda could not be found, but the man who went to Abu Talha found him and brought him; so he dug the grave of the apostle in the Medina fashion.

THE BURIAL OF THE APOSTLE

Then the men entered in throngs to pray for him. When they had completed their devotions the women came in; and when they had finished the children came. Yet no one had directed the people to visit the corpse of the apostle of Allah.

The apostle of Allah was buried in the middle of the night on Wednesday. Aisha said, 'We knew nothing about the burial of the apostle until we heard the sound of pickaxes in the middle of the night.' Those who went down into the grave of the apostle were the same men as washed the corpse. When the apostle had been laid in the grave and it was to be built up, his freed slave, Shuqran, took a wrapper which the apostle had used often and worn out; and, burying it in the grave, he said, 'No one shall wear it after thee.' It remained interred with the apostle.

According to Aisha, the apostle had said when he was dying, 'The curse of Allah is on a nation which makes the graves of its prophets into places of worship', but he knew that his own followers would do this. And it was true, for when the apostle died a great calamity befell the Muslims. Aisha, who survived the apostle forty-seven years, recorded, 'When the apostle of Allah died many Arabs relapsed into idolatry; Judaism and Christianity rose again, and Hypocrisy became common, so that the Muslims seemed like a flock of sheep on a wintry night, because of the loss of their prophet. Then Allah roused them again under Abu Bakr.'